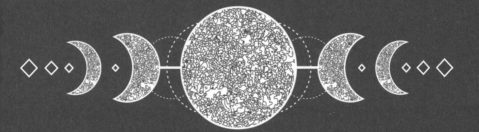

Moonology
Diary 2020

Yasmin Boland

HAY HOUSE

Carlsbad, California • New York City
London • Sydney • New Delhi

This diary belongs to

....

Published in the United Kingdom by:
Hay House UK Ltd, The Sixth Floor, Watson House,
54 Baker Street, London W1U 7BU
Tel: +44 (0)20 3927 7290; Fax: +44 (0)20 3927 7291
www.hayhouse.co.uk

Published in the United States of America by:
Hay House Inc., PO Box 5100, Carlsbad, CA 92018-5100
Tel: (1) 760 431 7695 or (800) 654 5126
Fax: (1) 760 431 6948 or (800) 650 5115
www.hayhouse.com

Published in Australia by:
Hay House Australia Ltd, 18/36 Ralph St, Alexandria NSW 2015
Tel: (61) 2 9669 4299; Fax: (61) 2 9669 4144
www.hayhouse.com.au

Published in India by:
Hay House Publishers India, Muskaan Complex, Plot No.3, B-2,
Vasant Kunj, New Delhi 110 070
Tel: (91) 11 4176 1620; Fax: (91) 11 4176 1630
www.hayhouse.co.in

A catalogue record for this book is available from the British Library.

ISBN: 978-1-78817-337-7

Interior images: 19 Nyx Rowan; all other illustrations WumiStudio/
Creative Market

Contents

Welcome to 2020!

Welcome to the *Moonology Diary 2020*! For those who choose to live consciously and work with the energies of the Moon, the year ahead is a gift. In addition to the 25 New and Full Moons, and some of the most powerful planetary energies for manifesting we've seen in a long time, 2020 begins with a Full Moon eclipse on 10 January and is followed by five further eclipses throughout the year. Eclipses are amazing times of change, so 2020 has the potential to be a big year for everyone!

Why work with the Moon? I've been teaching Moonology for 20 years and it's changed my life, and the lives of many others, in amazing ways. Living in alignment with the lunar cycle just works. Understanding how to work with the Moon is about knowing what to do when (or at least that's the minimum you need to know).

The high points of lunar energy every month are the New and Full Moon. If you do nothing else, work with them. At the New Moon, energies are rising, so this is the best time to set your intentions. The New Moon marks the beginning of the waxing cycle, which is a great time to start a new job, a love affair, or anything else. Full Moon marks the beginning of the waning cycle and is the time when energies are falling away. This is the best time to surrender and practise forgiveness, or let go of anything toxic, e.g. a relationship or a job you know isn't doing you any good.

Before we go further, here are a few notes for readers who are new to working with the lunar cycle.

Understanding the Lunar Cycle

One lunar cycle takes about 28 days and covers the time it takes for the Moon to complete one orbit of the Earth and move through Her eight main phases: New Moon (the traditional starting point), Crescent Moon, First Quarter Moon, Gibbous Moon, Full Moon, Disseminating Moon, Third Quarter Moon and Balsamic Moon.

The **New Moon** phase is the start of the waxing cycle when the Sun and the Moon are in the same place in the zodiac. You can't actually see the New Moon because She is positioned between the Earth and the Sun, and Her unilluminated side is therefore facing the Earth. For our purposes, this is the phase that also incorporates the Dark Moon, which is the moment before the New Moon. This is the time to get really clear in your intentions and to make some wishes as well, if you're so inclined!

The **Crescent Moon** phase occurs from $3\frac{1}{2}$ to 7 days after New Moon. The Moon has now separated from the Sun (overtaken on the zodiac, so to speak) and is now visible in the sky as a fine sliver. This is the time to really keep up the hard work on whatever you're manifesting. You should be hitting your stride.

The **First Quarter Moon** phase occurs from 7 to 10½ days after New Moon. This is when the Moon looks like a half-Moon and is a time when mini-crises can arise to test our commitment and resolve. It's all good!

The **Gibbous Moon** phase occurs from 10½ to 15 days after New Moon. I love to point out that 'Gibbous' means bulging. It's so evocative! The Moon is now bulging with our hopes and feelings, just ahead of the Full Moon.

The **Full Moon** phase occurs from 15 to 18½ days after New Moon and is the high point of the lunar cycle, one could argue. Our emotions come to the surface and it's a great time to deal with them. And we do, in this diary. This is also the time to practise forgiveness and release negativity.

The **Disseminating Moon** phase occurs from 3½ to 7 days after Full Moon and marks the start of the waning cycle. It's the time to release and move on. It's also the time to share what you've learned with others.

The **Third Quarter Moon** phase occurs from 7 to 10½ days after Full Moon. Again, the Moon looks like a half-Moon and again, there can be a mini-crises which are all reminding you to release whatever you need to release.

The **Balsamic Moon** phase begins roughly 10½ days after Full Moon and continues to the beginning of the New Moon. 'Balsamic' means healing and soothing. If something didn't work out it's time to make peace with it ahead of the coming New Moon. Life goes on and you can try again! Timing is everything and everything happens in Divine timing.

During the year, look to the heavens whenever you're out at night, or better yet, look at the Moon through a telescope – She's quite a sight to see!

Setting Goals at New Moon

I really hope that you'll use this diary to set your goals at every New Moon. It works, but you also have to *do* the work! This includes reading the text for each lunation, and filling in the write-in space with your lists of wishes and intentions. It's a way to unleash what you could call your 'sacred superpower'. Think of it as inspired, mystical, cosmic goal-setting, because it's a bit of all that. I can tell you with 100 per cent certainty that writing this very diary was *definitely* on my New Moon wish lists.

Goal-setting is always an amazing idea, but it's going to be huge this year because Capricorn, the ambitious goal-setting sign, is where so much energy is throughout the year.

Practising Forgiveness at Full Moon

Conversely, Full Moon is a time of heightened emotions, for climaxes and conclusions, and when you receive answers, including to questions posed at the previous New Moon. The Full Moon is also an important time for forgiveness, to practise gratitude and to release negativity. The sign the Full Moon is in can also be used to support any efforts you're making to live consciously and in tune with the Universe.

To help enhance your journey with this diary I've created meditations for you to download and use at each

New and Full Moon. Just visit moonmessages.com/diarymeditations. Filling out the New Moon intentions and Full Moon forgiveness sections *after* listening to these meditations will make for a more heart-based, heart-felt, heart-led experience.

Signs of the Zodiac

As you work through this diary over the course of the year, you'll see that the New and Full Moons unfold in a regular and predictable order – essentially, they work through the 12 signs of the zodiac in the same order as you would read Star signs in a newspaper horoscope: Aries, Taurus, Gemini, Cancer, Leo, Virgo, Libra, Scorpio, Sagittarius, Capricorn, Aquarius and Pisces.

Aries	♈	Libra	♎
Taurus	♉	Scorpio	♏
Gemini	♊	Sagittarius	♐
Cancer	♋	Capricorn	♑
Leo	♌	Aquarius	♒
Virgo	♍	Pisces	♓

My aim for this diary is to take you, the reader, the possible non-astrologer, or astro-newbie or fully fledged astrologer, on a journey with the Moon. Expect heat, lessons, eruptions, volatility, lots of ambitions and success, and to get somewhere at freaking last! Also expect practical magick.

Manifesting with the New Moon

If you have a goal you want to manifest – from a new bike to a new lover to a new spiritual teacher – this is a year for conscious creating and creative visualization. The energies are so high.

Call me idealistic, but I hope that by the time you read this, a year on from the time of writing, manifestation and creative visualization will be considered more mainstream. In my opinion, that we can manifest our lives is already proven – elite athletes, for instance, have known about and used the power of visualization to achieve goals for decades. I feel it's now time for everyone else to get on board. And the Capricorn energy around this year might be just what we need to make that happen! So that we can test it together, I'm offering you, readers of this diary, free membership to my closed Facebook group, which you can join by visiting moonmessages.com/pfg. See you there!

The year ahead brings many practical (Saturn) magick (Pluto) energies and six eclipses, which means it's a great year to focus on manifesting. Being aware of these energies is part of living consciously.

What Does It Mean to Live Consciously?

For me, a large part of living consciously means living with the Moon and the planets as cosmic timers, and being aware of our actions and patterns. If you've dabbled with conscious creation, especially if you've done this in tune with the Moon, then you'll know how this works and how powerful it can be. If not, get ready to learn!

One of the most difficult lessons to learn about manifestation and conscious creation is that it has to come from the heart, not the ego. When we manifest, we get back what we 'put out', so if you manifest from your ego, then in fact you might not receive what you want because it's not what your *heart* truly desires. This is *so* important, and why all good teachers will tell you that manifesting has to come from the heart – because the heart knows!

Think Good Thoughts

The next thing to understand is that manifesting comes through our feelings. How we feel about someone or something is what we manifest, which is why it's important not to worry all the time! I'm not advocating that you only think happy thoughts and say happy words in 2020, or any other year for that matter. I'm saying that the more your natural mindset is happy, the better. As they say, good thoughts lead to good deeds, lead to good karma!

How does this relate to the Moon? Well, we manifest through our feelings and emotions, and guess what the Moon is all about in astrology? Feelings and emotions. As She moves through Her phases, Her effect can bring our feelings and heightened emotions to the surface. If we can harness Her different energies at the right time *and* manifest from the heart, we should be able to consciously create our lives.

Where's My Stuff?

Before we go any further, let's talk about what we can manifest. The truth is that we can manifest anything, really. We already do. Everything that we have created started as an idea. In Moonology, we aim to create consciously rather than unconsciously, and once you've mastered the art, you can probably manifest a new car as easily as you can manifest a home-delivery pizza, but maybe not quite as fast!

But should you?

Yes, you should!

Consider the idea that the Earth is a school of manifestation (thank you, Sonia Choquette, for explaining this to me), and that we incarnate here to learn about how to consciously create. Then go one step further, to an interplanetary and interdimensional level, and consider that we're multidimensional beings, and a part of us is attached to what we call our Higher Self, and a part of us is here on Earth to learn how to manifest. In this diary, we'll manifest 'for the good of all or not at all'!

Just be aware that all sorts of earthly things, such as self-doubt, addiction, envy, jealousy, processed food, pollutants and so on can keep us stuck and block our ability to manifest. This is yet another reason why we need to wake up and be conscious about our thoughts and actions, and even our environment.

Full Moon Forgiveness

As you work with this diary, you'll notice that we focus on the positive and what we want rather than the negative and what we don't want, but we'll also *deal* with the negative. This is particularly relevant at Full Moon, which is the best time to practise forgiveness and self-forgiveness. Not only does forgiveness clear away karma, but it also breaks the ties between you and whatever or whoever happened to you. Remember, though, that forgiveness must come from the heart.

Let's begin with my favourite forgiveness prose, adapted from the *A Forgiveness Formula* by Catherine Ponder and reproduced below with her kind permission. Read it out loud... now... tonight... tomorrow night... whenever you need to forgive yourself or someone else... but it's especially powerful at Full Moon.

> *'Under the glorious Full Moon, I forgive everything,*
> *everyone, every experience, every memory of*
> *the past or present that needs forgiveness. I*
> *forgive positively everyone. I also forgive myself*
> *of past mistakes. The Universe is love, and I am*
> *forgiven and governed by love alone. Love is now*
> *adjusting my life. Realizing this, I abide in peace.*

'I bring love and healing to all my thoughts, beliefs and relationships. I learn my lessons and move on. I call on my soul fragments to be cleansed by the Full Moon and I call on them to rejoin me. I send love to myself and everyone I know, and everyone who knows me, in all directions of time. Under this glorious Full Moon, I am healed. My life is healed. And so it is. So be it.'

As with manifesting, any time is a good time to forgive someone (even if we don't forget). But the Full Moon is especially good, because all of our emotions bubble up and are therefore easier to tune in to and process. So, at this time, think about whether you're happy or sad, and why, then work with it and recite the forgiveness formula.

At the time of the Full Moon, the keyword is 'Surrender'. Surrender to your Higher Self, to the Universe, to God/dess. Acknowledge that there are some things we don't understand yet. Accept what is and sit with that... then give yourself time out during the waning cycle, which will lead you back to... New Moon and the next waxing cycle.

This diary also includes resistance work for you to do during the year. This means working out why you're resisting change. So, for example, on the most basic level, if you think rich people are evil, you will resist abundance! Resistance work also helps to give you an energetic clear-out so that you can more easily send out your 'cosmic orders' from your heart and consciously create your best life.

Key Lunar Events This Year

A s I mentioned earlier, this year will bring some of the most powerful planetary energies we've seen in a long time. Here is an overview of key events:

New and Full Moons of 2020

For each lunation, I've listed the time of the New and Full Moon in London, Sydney, Los Angeles and New York. To find out the time at any other location, visit moonmessages.com /moontimes.

Full Moon eclipse in Cancer			New Moon in Aquarius		
London	10 Jan	19:21	London	24 Jan	21:42
Sydney	11 Jan	06:21	Sydney	25 Jan	08:42
Los Angeles	10 Jan	11:21	Los Angeles	24 Jan	13:42
New York	10 Jan	14:21	New York	24 Jan	16:42
Full Moon in Leo			New Moon in Pisces		
London	9 Feb	07:33	London	23 Feb	15:32
Sydney	9 Feb	18:33	Sydney	24 Feb	02:32
Los Angeles	8 Feb	23:33	Los Angeles	23 Feb	07:32
New York	9 Feb	02:33	New York	23 Feb	10:32

Super Full Moon in Virgo			New Moon in Aries		
London	9 Mar	17:47	London	24 Mar	09:28
Sydney	10 Mar	04:47	Sydney	24 Mar	20:28
Los Angeles	9 Mar	10:47	Los Angeles	24 Mar	02:28
New York	9 Mar	13:47	New York	24 Mar	05:28
Super Full Moon in Libra			New Moon in Taurus		
London	8 Apr	03:35	London	23 Apr	03:25
Sydney	8 Apr	12:35	Sydney	23 Apr	12:25
Los Angeles	7 Apr	19:35	Los Angeles	22 Apr	19:25
New York	7 Apr	22:35	New York	22 Apr	22:25
Full Moon in Scorpio			New Moon in Gemini		
London	7 May	11:45	London	22 May	18:38
Sydney	7 May	20:45	Sydney	23 May	03:38
Los Angeles	7 May	03:45	Los Angeles	22 May	10:38
New York	7 May	06:45	New York	22 May	13:38
Full Moon eclipse in Sagittarius			New Moon eclipse in Cancer		
London	5 Jun	20:12	London	21 Jun	07:41
Sydney	6 Jun	05:12	Sydney	21 Jun	16:41
Los Angeles	5 Jun	12:12	Los Angeles	20 Jun	23:41
New York	5 Jun	15:12	New York	21 Jun	02:41
Full Moon eclipse in Capricorn			New Moon in Cancer		
London	5 Jul	05:44	London	20 Jul	18:32
Sydney	5 Jul	14:44	Sydney	21 Jul	03:32
Los Angeles	4 Jul	21:44	Los Angeles	20 Jul	10:32
New York	5 Jul	00:44	New York	20 Jul	13:32

Full Moon in Aquarius			New Moon in Leo		
London	3 Aug	16:58	London	19 Aug	03:41
Sydney	4 Aug	01:58	Sydney	19 Aug	12:41
Los Angeles	3 Aug	08:58	Los Angeles	18 Aug	19:41
New York	3 Aug	11:58	New York	18 Aug	22:41
Full Moon in Pisces			New Moon in Virgo		
London	2 Sep	06:22	London	17 Sep	12:00
Sydney	2 Sep	15:22	Sydney	17 Sep	21:00
Los Angeles	1 Sep	22:22	Los Angeles	17 Sep	04:00
New York	2 Sep	01:22	New York	17 Sep	07:00
Full Moon in Aries			Super New Moon in Libra		
London	1 Oct	22:05	London	16 Oct	20:31
Sydney	2 Oct	07:05	Sydney	17 Oct	06:31
Los Angeles	1 Oct	14:05	Los Angeles	16 Oct	12:31
New York	1 Oct	17:05	New York	16 Oct	15:31
Full Moon in Taurus			Super New Moon in Scorpio		
London	31 Oct	14:49	London	15 Nov	05:07
Sydney	1 Nov	01:49	Sydney	15 Nov	16:07
Los Angeles	31 Oct	07:49	Los Angeles	14 Nov	21:07
New York	31 Oct	10:49	New York	15 Nov	00:07
Full Moon eclipse in Gemini			New Moon eclipse in Sagittarius		
London	30 Nov	09:29	London	14 Dec	16:16
Sydney	30 Nov	20:29	Sydney	15 Dec	03:16
Los Angeles	30 Nov	01:29	Los Angeles	14 Dec	08:16
New York	30 Nov	04:29	New York	14 Dec	11:16

Full Moon in Cancer			New Moon in Capricorn		
London	30 Dec	03:28	London	13 Jan	05:00
Sydney	30 Dec	14:28	Sydney	13 Jan	16:00
Los Angeles	29 Dec	19:28	Los Angeles	12 Jan	21:00
New York	29 Dec	22:28	New York	13 Jan	00:00

Eclipses

An eclipse is a karmic event that happens when the passage of the Moon around the Earth connects with the passage of the Earth around the Sun. Traditionally, eclipses represent where we've come from – our past lives – or where we need to go to find happiness and fulfilment – the development our soul needs.

At an eclipse, the Universe changes gears. Eclipses open and close portals. They represent a moment in time when we can jump from one life to another, like a game in which two sliding doors need to be in alignment so that we can walk through them. In this game, the doorways are represented by the north and south nodes – the points at which the Moon's orbital path crosses the ecliptic (the Sun's apparent yearly path on the celestial sphere). The south node represents karma and the north node represents potential. So, for instance, if you're clinging on to a relationship that you know is over, at the time of an eclipse, something might happen to enable you to move on once and for all.

We'll see six eclipses this year, one less than the maximum possible. In this diary I give times for London, Sydney, Los Angeles and New York, so when a date below spans 2 days it reflects the same moment in different time zones:

10–11 January	Full Moon eclipse in Cancer
5–6 June	Full Moon eclipse in Sagittarius
20–21 June	New Moon eclipse in Cancer
4–5 July	Full Moon eclipse in Capricorn
30 November	Full Moon eclipse in Gemini
14–15 December	New Moon eclipse in Sagittarius

At the time of each eclipse I'll give interpretations and ideas for working with its energies. If an eclipse falls a few days before or after your birthday, then expect a memorable year (especially if it's a few days before your birthday, as this means it's triggering your Star sign). Also, if your half-birthday happens to fall either side of an eclipse, the eclipse would be right opposite your Sun and therefore also important, especially in the event of a Full Moon eclipse.

I think of eclipses as mood enhancers, so if your life is going well, it can feel even better in the weeks before and after the eclipse. Of course, if things aren't going so well, the opposite can also be true.

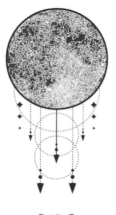

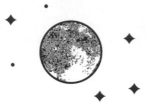

Working with the Houses

In addition to manifesting and practising forgiveness, we also work with the New and Full Moons to make predictions. Each New and Full Moon triggers a part of your astrological chart called a House. A simple way to make predictions is to work out which House the New or Full Moon is triggering in your chart. Then, just refer to the quick guide below to give you an idea of what each lunation means for you.

All you need to know is your Star sign, or better yet your Rising sign. Your Star sign is good for a quick fix – what you read regarding the House your Star sign triggers should resonate with you. However, your Rising sign is based on your time, date and place of birth, so the House triggered by your Rising sign each month will be much more accurate in terms of what to focus on. If you don't know your Rising sign, visit moonmessages.com/freechart. You will be sent your chart and details of your Rising sign. Keep this safe so that you can refer back to it at each lunation.

A Quick Guide to the Houses

The 1st House: your appearance and image; self-identity; how you come across to others.

The 2nd House: money, property and possessions; values, including how you value yourself.

The 3rd House: communications; siblings; neighbours; quick trips; early learning and education.

The 4th House: home and family, all things domestic; where you belong; your past.

The 5th House: romance; creativity; kids (your own or someone else's); pursuit of pleasure; love affairs.

The 6th House: daily routines, including at work; your health; duty.

The 7th House: your lovers; your spouse; your ex; enemies; any sort of partner, including business partners; cooperation and competition.

The 8th House: joint finances; credit cards; debts; sex; anything you consider taboo; inheritance; transformation.

The 9th House: study; travel; the Great Cosmic Quest; the Internet; higher learning; religion; teaching, spirituality.

The 10th House: your career and ambitions; how you make your mark on the world: what you're known for; your reputation.

The 11th House: friends; networks; social circles; hopes and wishes.

The 12th House: your fears; your spirituality; dreams; self-undoing; withdrawal; secret or hidden enemies. This is the deepest, darkest, most sensitive part of your chart.

Suggested Ways to Use This Diary

One of the things that surprised me when the *Moonology Diary 2019* came out was the number of people who contacted me to ask, 'What should I write in the daily spaces on the diary pages?' I write all of my appointments and important dates here, but realize this might be considered old-school in an era when so many of us use electronic diaries! So here are a few things you could record each day if you don't want to use the space for appointments:

- A daily gratitude note. The more grateful you are, the more you will have to be grateful for!

- Notes about your New Moon wishes, or what you want to release and surrender at Full Moon.

- A thought for the day.

- A quote that strikes a chord with you.

- A message from an oracle card or Tarot reading.

- A visualization doodle.

It really is up to you! I'd love to know how you use the space, so please feel free to email me at diary@moonology.com.

Weekly
Diary

JANUARY

M	T	W	T	F	S	S
		1	2	3	4	5
6	7	8	9	10	11	12
13	14	15	16	17	18	19
20	21	22	23	24	25	26
27	28	29	30	31		

FEBRUARY

M	T	W	T	F	S	S
					1	2
3	4	5	6	7	8	9
10	11	12	13	14	15	16
17	18	19	20	21	22	23
24	25	26	27	28	29	

MARCH

M	T	W	T	F	S	S
						1
2	3	4	5	6	7	8
9	10	11	12	13	14	15
16	17	18	19	20	21	22
23	24	25	26	27	28	29
30	31					

APRIL

M	T	W	T	F	S	S
		1	2	3	4	5
6	7	8	9	10	11	12
13	14	15	16	17	18	19
20	21	22	23	24	25	26
27	28	29	30			

MAY

M	T	W	T	F	S	S
				1	2	3
4	5	6	7	8	9	10
11	12	13	14	15	16	17
18	19	20	21	22	23	24
25	26	27	28	29	30	31

JUNE

M	T	W	T	F	S	S
1	2	3	4	5	6	7
8	9	10	11	12	13	14
15	16	17	18	19	20	21
22	23	24	25	26	27	28
29	30					

JULY

M	T	W	T	F	S	S
		1	2	3	4	5
6	7	8	9	10	11	12
13	14	15	16	17	18	19
20	21	22	23	24	25	26
27	28	29	30	31		

AUGUST

M	T	W	T	F	S	S
					1	2
3	4	5	6	7	8	9
10	11	12	13	14	15	16
17	18	19	20	21	22	23
24	25	26	27	28	29	30
31						

SEPTEMBER

M	T	W	T	F	S	S
	1	2	3	4	5	6
7	8	9	10	11	12	13
14	15	16	17	18	19	20
21	22	23	24	25	26	27
28	29	30				

OCTOBER

M	T	W	T	F	S	S
			1	2	3	4
5	6	7	8	9	10	11
12	13	14	15	16	17	18
19	20	21	22	23	24	25
26	27	28	29	30	31	

NOVEMBER

M	T	W	T	F	S	S
						1
2	3	4	5	6	7	8
9	10	11	12	13	14	15
16	17	18	19	20	21	22
23	24	25	26	27	28	29
30						

DECEMBER

M	T	W	T	F	S	S
	1	2	3	4	5	6
7	8	9	10	11	12	13
14	15	16	17	18	19	20
21	22	23	24	25	26	27
28	29	30	31			

DECEMBER 2019 WEEK 52

---

23 MONDAY

---

24 TUESDAY

---

25 WEDNESDAY

New Moon eclipse
Los Angeles   21:12

---

26 THURSDAY

New Moon eclipse
London   05:12
Sydney   16:12
New York   00:12

 ♑

FRIDAY 27

● ♑♒

SATURDAY 28

● ♒

SUNDAY 29

This Week

*It's the last full week of the year and it ends with a New Moon
eclipse! Make the most of it and set your 2020 intentions now!*

January

Expect the year to start with very high energies! On 10 January comes a Full Moon eclipse in the sign of Cancer, which is going to be both emotional and a time to release and let go of whatever you're clinging on to. Are you ready? To make some magic, begin under this Full Moon by surrendering 2020 to the Divine.

There is also a major alignment between Saturn and Pluto in Capricorn, marking several of the key themes of the year ahead – streamlining the way you work, learning

Full Moon eclipse in Cancer		
London	10 Jan	19:21
Sydney	11 Jan	06:21
Los Angeles	10 Jan	11:21
New York	10 Jan	14:21
New Moon in Aquarius		
London	24 Jan	21:42
Sydney	25 Jan	08:42
Los Angeles	24 Jan	13:42
New York	24 Jan	16.42

lessons that can transform your life and facing facts about where change is needed or inevitable. All in all, it's a good start for 2020! As January begins, ask yourself what you're grateful for and decide on your biggest aim for the month.

M	T	W	T	F	S	S
		1	2	3 ◑	4	5
6	7	8	9	10 ○	11	12
13	14	15	16	17 ◐	18	19
20	21	22	23	24 ●	25	26
27	28	29	30	31		

～ Things to do this month ～

1. Chant 'Om Namo Narayani' (I surrender to the Divine).
2. *Really* release 2019 – just let it go!
3. Show someone how much they mean to you.

Dec/Jan Week 1

---

30 MONDAY

---

31 TUESDAY

---

1 WEDNESDAY ♓︎◗

---

2 THURSDAY

FRIDAY 3

What are you grateful for right now?

SATURDAY 4

SUNDAY 5

THIS WEEK

Happy New Year! Start 2020 as you mean to go on.
Want to get into meditation, live more healthily or
manifest effectively? Begin your practice now!

Full Moon Eclipse in Cancer

Are you sure you've released 2019?

London	10 January	19:21
Sydney	11 January	06:21
Los Angeles	10 January	11:21
New York	10 January	14:21

This is a massive week astrologically, and as it's the start of the year life is already energetically charged. We're getting a Full Moon and it's an eclipse. This means the energies are hyper and we have plenty to play with as we move into the start of the year.

Energetically, if you want to consciously create your life in 2020, you need to be clear in your head and heart. If your head is full of self-doubt and in your heart you feel you're not worthy, then this Full Moon eclipse is the time to work on that. You won't manifest anything you don't feel completely worthy of. It's that simple. So think about why you feel unworthy and who needs to be forgiven for any self-doubt to go away.

Under the Full Moon, light a candle and perform a forgiveness ceremony in which you sit and think about who you need to forgive. This might include yourself. Have you been holding on to hurt? Can you let it go? Would you let it go if you knew it meant you could start to manifest your best life? Write down the names of those you're forgiving and burn the list, then read the *A Forgiveness Formula* (see page 9). Also remember to be grateful for all you have.

ⵣ What This Lunation Means for You

There could be some issues arising in the part of your chart being triggered, but they're just challenges to see how determined you are to make 2020 an amazing year. Find your Rising sign in this list to discover which House the Moon is in for you (see page 16 for a quick guide): Aries – 4th House; Taurus – 3rd House; Gemini – 2nd House; Cancer – 1st House; Leo – 12th House; Virgo – 11th House; Libra – 10th House; Scorpio – 9th House; Sagittarius – 8th House; Capricorn – 7th House; Aquarius – 6th House; Pisces – 5th House.

ⵣ Talk to the Moon

On the night before or after the Full Moon (either is fine) go outside and look at the Moon. If you can't go outside, look at Her from indoors. Contemplate the idea that She has a highly emotional frequency. Feel Her loving moonbeams. Visualize them flooding your aura and chakras. The Moon represents the Divine Mother and Sacred Feminine, so talk to Her about your feelings.

If you can't see the Moon, it's easiest to visualize Her as a Full Moon. Use soft lighting, play beautiful music, light a beeswax candle or burn an essential oil; it can still be a beautiful experience.

Full Moon Forgiveness List

Full Moon is an important time for forgiveness, to practise gratitude and to release negativity. What do you need to let go of this month? Who do you need to forgive? What or whom do you need to practise gratitude for?

Visit moonmessages.com/diarymeditations to listen to the Moon meditation for this month, ideally before you make your list below. This will enable you to write from the heart.

_____

_____

_____

_____

_____

_____

_____

_____

_____

_____

Questions to Ask at This Full Moon

Are my insecurities holding me back, and if so, what am I going to do about it?

Am I reluctant to change, and if so, why?

What do I really want to leave behind in 2019 that I haven't yet cut ties with (and am I ready to cut those ties)?

JANUARY WEEK 2

....

6 MONDAY   ♉︎ ☾

....

7 TUESDAY   ♉︎♊︎ ◐

....

8 WEDNESDAY   ♊︎ ◐

....

9 THURSDAY   ♊︎♋︎ ◯

....

○ ♋

FRIDAY 10

Full Moon eclipse
London   19:21
Los Angeles   11:21
New York   14:21

○ ♋♌

SATURDAY 11

Full Moon eclipse
Sydney   06:21

○ ♌

SUNDAY 12

THIS WEEK

*This week is absolutely ripe for powerful change owing to a meeting
of Saturn and Pluto, which happens only once in every 30 or so
years. Use the opportunity or lose it. You say you want a revolution?*

JANUARY WEEK 3

....

13 MONDAY   ♌ ♍ ○

....

14 TUESDAY   ♍ ○

....

15 WEDNESDAY   ♍ ♎ ◐

....

16 THURSDAY   ♎ ◑

....

 FRIDAY 17

What are you grateful for right now?

 SATURDAY 18

☽♏︎♐ SUNDAY 19

THIS WEEK

This is a week to get serious, but good things related
to love and money might happen quickly.

New Moon in Aquarius

This week heralds Chinese New Year and 'Woke Folk'.

London	24 January	21:42
Sydney	25 January	08:42
Los Angeles	24 January	13:42
New York	24 January	16:42

The heavens sent me the following quote from Emilia Carlotta Caverzasio, which is perfect for this week's New Moon: *'The process of becoming a conscious manifestor is, at the end of the day, a process of awakening. You're awakening to your true self: the role of Creator in this world. We are all creators, we are here to create, not to learn.'*

Aquarius is the sign that wakes us all up. It's for forward-thinking people, such as yourself, who know they have the ability to manifest their dreams and aren't afraid to use their powers. So what are you manifesting this month, as we move further into the new year?

The first planetary alignment after the New Moon is between Mercury and Mars, which makes this a great time to surprise people by speaking up for yourself. Remember that you're on a conscious creation ride this year. Are you ready to start? The New Moon is always the time to 'do the work' and this first New Moon of the year is that plus plus!

As the quote on the previous page says, the process of becoming a conscious manifestor is a process of awakening to your true self. The question to ask at this positive New Moon in Aquarius is: What are you drawing into your life?

⚹ What This Lunation Means for You

This New Moon looks very friendly and kind, so whatever is happening in the part of your chart you read about should be very pleasant. Find your Rising sign in this list to discover which House the Moon is in for you (see page 16 for a quick guide): Aries – 11th House; Taurus – 10th House; Gemini – 9th House; Cancer – 8th House; Leo – 7th House; Virgo – 6th House; Libra – 5th House; Scorpio – 4th House; Sagittarius – 3rd House; Capricorn – 2nd House; Aquarius – 1st House; Pisces – 12th House.

⚹ Connect with White Tara

This a wonderful week to work with the energies of the Goddess White Tara. Honour her with a lush floral arrangement in your home (preferably on your altar). Mix foliage with white flowers of any kind. Ask her to help you to speed things along in the conscious creation process, and to help keep your mind fresh and open to new ideas.

White Tara is known as the 'mother of liberation' and the energy of Aquarius is all about being liberated, to the point of being detached. Where in your life do you need to liberate yourself so you can manifest your dreams? Ask White Tara for help in this area.

New Moon Wishes and Intentions

What are you manifesting this New Moon? Before you make your list of dreams and desires, visit moonmessages.com/diarymeditations and listen to the Moon meditation for this month. This will enable you to think from the heart – the best place to be. Then go through your list and 'feel' each wish as real, or feel the feeling of it being fulfilled.

_____

_____

_____

_____

_____

_____

_____

_____

_____

_____

_____

☍ Questions to Ask at This New Moon

Name three things I want to happen quickly.

_____

_____

_____

_____

How likely do I think it is that each thing listed above will happen? Give a percentage for each.

_____

_____

_____

_____

How do I raise that percentage (if it's less than 90 per cent)?

_____

_____

_____

_____

_____

JANUARY Week 4

20 MONDAY

21 TUESDAY

22 WEDNESDAY

23 THURSDAY

New Moon ♑ ♒   FRIDAY 24

New Moon
London   21:42
Los Angeles   13:42
New York   16:42

New Moon ♒   SATURDAY 25

New Moon
Sydney   08:42

New Moon ♒ ♓   SUNDAY 26

THIS WEEK

*The New Moon in Aquarius ushers in the Chinese New
Year, so a big Kung Hei Fat Choy to you and yours!*

February

It's Valentine's month, so what can you expect? The planetary combo influencing 14 February this year is between lucky Jupiter and dreamy Neptune, so whether you're single or in love and looking forward to a super-romantic Valentine's Day, the energy is positive.

For singles who are open to love, 14–19 February is a great time to make a wish list and set intentions about what you want for yourself in your next relationship. For loved-up couples, dreams of taking your relationship to

Full Moon in Leo		
London	9 February	07:33
Sydney	9 February	18:33
Los Angeles	8 February	23:33
New York	9 February	02:33
New Moon in Pisces		
London	23 February	15:32
Sydney	24 February	02:32
Los Angeles	23 February	07:32
New York	23 February	10:32

the next level can come true now. And if you're over love and never want to be in another relationship? Use 14–19 February to make a wish list or a vision board about what you *do* want for your future.

M	T	W	T	F	S	S
					1	2
3	4	5	6	7	8	9
10	11	12	13	14	15	16
17	18	19	20	21	22	23
24	25	26	27	28	29	

~ *Things to do this month* ~

1. Practise creative visualization.
2. Back up your computer before 18 February (Mercury retrograde begins).
3. Recommit to your spiritual path.

Jan/Feb Week 5

....

27 Monday

....

28 Tuesday

....

29 Wednesday

....

30 Thursday

....

FRIDAY 31

SATURDAY 1

Festivals of Imbolc (UK/USA) and Lammas (Aus)

O♈ SUNDAY 2

What are you grateful for right now?

THIS WEEK

You may experience some weirdness this week, thanks to a slightly strange Mars–Neptune clash. Be reassured it will pass!

Full Moon in Leo

Make this a healing Full Moon.

London	9 February	07:33
Sydney	9 February	18:33
Los Angeles	8 February	23:33
New York	9 February	02:33

This week brings the Full Moon in Leo, so it's time to release pride. Pay attention: is pride derailing you? If you know your pride is getting in your way, then work on that. Leo, pride and the dreaded ego all go hand in hand. Although we need a healthy ego, we don't need it to take over our life. So think about that this week, especially if you have an upset with someone. Upsets at the time of the Full Moon are of course more common since emotions come to the surface as the Moon swells to fullness.

Now is also the time of the month to surrender. If you don't want to surrender to the Divine, at least surrender to your Higher Self! There's also a strong healing vibration in the air this week, as just after the Full Moon we get a link between Venus (the planet of love, caresses and femininity) and Chiron (the healing planetoid). If you've fallen out with someone you really care for, now is the time to reach out and make peace, especially if pride has been getting in your way! Remember that once the Full Moon has been and gone we move into the waning cycle, which is the time to release and let go.

ⵣ What This Lunation Means for You

Where are issues building for you this month? There could be drama in the part of your life being triggered, so stay focused on your goals. Find your Rising sign in this list to discover which House the Moon is in for you (see page 16 for a quick guide): Aries – 5th House; Taurus – 4th House; Gemini – 3rd House; Cancer – 2nd House; Leo – 1st House; Virgo – 12th House; Libra – 11th House; Scorpio – 10th House; Sagittarius – 9th House; Capricorn – 8th House; Aquarius – 7th House; Pisces – 6th House.

ⵣ Reignite Your Self-Belief

Full Moon in a fire sign is the time to work with fire in any rituals or ceremonies to express outwardly whatever is going on energetically. So, light a red candle this month, and think of it burning away any pride that's been causing issues. If you're low on pride, use the candle to relight and reignite your self-belief and self-love. Forgive whomever made you feel less than great, or not good enough, in the past. They were there to push your buttons so that you could rise above and evolve. If you like to work with angels, Archangel Raziel, the technicolour angel who likes to make an entrance (like any good Leo!), is the one to talk to.

Full Moon Forgiveness List

Full Moon is an important time for forgiveness, to practise gratitude and to release negativity. What do you need to let go of this month? Who do you need to forgive? What or whom do you need to practise gratitude for?

Visit moonmessages.com/diarymeditations to listen to the Moon meditation for this month, ideally before you make your list below. This will enable you to write from the heart.

_____

_____

_____

_____

_____

_____

_____

_____

_____

_____

⸸ Questions to Ask at This Full Moon

Have I let pride get in my way? If so, when?

_____

_____

_____

_____

Who do I need to forgive, but my pride is stopping me?

_____

_____

_____

_____

Releasing upset doesn't make what happened okay, it just means I can move on. How will I know I've moved on?

_____

_____

_____

_____

_____

FEBRUARY WEEK 6

3 MONDAY

4 TUESDAY ♊🌑

5 WEDNESDAY ♊♋🌑

6 THURSDAY ♋🌑

◯ ♋ ♌

FRIDAY 7

◯ ♌

SATURDAY 8

Full Moon
Los Angeles   23:33

◯ ♌ ♍

SUNDAY 9

Full Moon
London   07:33
Sydney   18:33
New York   02:33

THIS WEEK

The Goddess I work with under Leo energies is the amazing
Medusa. She represents the decapitation of the matriarchy
by the patriarchy, hence why she's seen as scary!

FEBRUARY Week 7

10 MONDAY ♍ ○

11 TUESDAY ♍♎ ○

12 WEDNESDAY ♎ ○

13 THURSDAY ♎ ○

 FRIDAY 14

 SATURDAY 15

What are you grateful for right now?

 **SUNDAY 16**

THIS WEEK

*Valentine's Day on 14 February falls in the waning
cycle, so even though the energies are good, they might
be a little more subdued than you hoped for…*

New Moon in Pisces

It's time to commit to your spiritual practice.

London	23 February	15:32
Sydney	24 February	02:32
Los Angeles	23 February	07:32
New York	23 February	10:32

This is a potentially amazing week, especially for manifesting. We have the New Moon in the sign of Pisces, *and* an amazing link between Jupiter and Neptune. This is what you might call an astrological super-whammy, because Jupiter (expansion or good luck) and Neptune (dreams) are both associated with the sign of Pisces; in fact, Jupiter and Neptune guide Pisces. Jupiter is about the big picture, higher learning that expands the mind and perspective, while Neptune is about dreams, poetry and the Divine. Add them to dreamy, psychic and spiritual Pisces, and you have the makings of a very blessed New Moon!

One of the best ways to use the energies is to think about your spiritual practice. Is this something you want for yourself this year? If so, the New Moon in Pisces is a particularly good time to begin or renew your commitment.

✸ What This Lunation Means for You

Find your Rising sign in this list to discover which House the Moon is in for you (see page 16 for a quick guide): Aries – 12th House; Taurus – 11th House; Gemini – 10th House; Cancer – 9th House; Leo – 8th House; Virgo – 7th House; Libra – 6th House; Scorpio – 5th House; Sagittarius – 4th House; Capricorn – 3rd House; Aquarius – 2nd House; Pisces – 1st House.

✸ My Spiritual Practices

Make a list of spiritual practices that most appeal – yoga, meditation, chanting, Tarot, manifesting, magick, working with oracle cards, tai chi, Reiki, etc. I have filled in #3 for you!

1. _____

2. _____

3. Connecting with the magical Moon!

Now that you've decided what you'd like to do, you need to commit to doing it.

I _____ do hereby commit to doing what I love spiritually, on a regular basis from here on in.

Can you see how this works? You get clear, you make the commitment and then you will start to manifest, assuming it's what you really want. The Moon is one of the very best spiritual companions that a magical spiritual quester could ask for. There She is up in the sky and Her movements through the lunar cycle serve as the perfect framework for your practices!

New Moon Wishes and Intentions

What are you manifesting this New Moon? Before you make your list of dreams and desires, visit moonmessages.com/diarymeditations and listen to the Moon meditation for this month. This will enable you to think from the heart – the best place to be. Then go through your list and 'feel' each wish as real, or feel the feeling of it being fulfilled.

_____

_____

_____

_____

_____

_____

_____

_____

_____

_____

_____

⚴ Questions to Ask at This New Moon

How can I live as a conscious person in 2020?

_____

_____

_____

_____

What does a consciously lived life look like?

_____

_____

_____

_____

How can I recommit to my favourite spiritual practice?

_____

_____

_____

_____

_____

FEBRUARY WEEK 8

17 MONDAY

18 TUESDAY

Mercury goes retrograde (until 10 March).

19 WEDNESDAY

20 THURSDAY

FRIDAY 21

SATURDAY 22

● ♒ ♓

SUNDAY 23

New Moon
London   15:32
Los Angeles 07:32
New York   10:32

THIS WEEK

This week sees the start of the first Mercury retrograde of the year. This time around it's in the same place as this week's New Moon, Pisces. Mercury retrograde is often thought of as a time when things go wrong, but things can just as easily go right!

FEBRUARY Week 9

24 MONDAY

New Moon
Sydney   02:32

25 TUESDAY

26 WEDNESDAY

27 THURSDAY

 FRIDAY 28

 SATURDAY 29

◐♉♊ SUNDAY 1

THIS WEEK

Mercury reverses and connects harmoniously with the
Sun, Mars and Uranus, making this a good time to
have a conversation you've been putting off.

March

This month brings the New Moon in Aries, the first sign of the zodiac, which is a kind of astrological new year. As such, it's a time to make the most of! If you've already fallen off the bandwagon when it comes to your aims and resolutions for 2020, this is the ideal time to start all over again. Of course, you can start over every day, but this is an especially powerful time energetically to do that.

Since you're a Moon lover, use the Aries energies to commit to working with the Moon every month for the next

Super Full Moon in Virgo		
London	9 March	17:47
Sydney	10 March	04:47
Los Angeles	9 March	10:47
New York	9 March	13:47
New Moon in Aries		
London	24 March	09:28
Sydney	24 March	20:28
Los Angeles	24 March	02:28
New York	24 March	05:28

12 months, too. It really will change your life for the better! As March begins, remember to think about what you're grateful for in your life and decide on your biggest aim for the month ahead.

M	T	W	T	F	S	S
						1
2 ◑	3	4	5	6	7	8
9 ○	10	11	12	13	14	15
16 ◐	17	18	19	20	21	22
23	24 ●	25	26	27	28	29
30	31					

～ Things to do this month ～

1. Write a list of what you want to achieve in 2020.

2. Take inspired action a few days after 10 March when Mercury retrograde ends.

3. See what life lessons are coming your way as Saturn leaves Capricorn and dips his toes into Aquarius.

MARCH WEEK 10

. . . .

2 MONDAY

What are you grateful for right now?
. . . .

3 TUESDAY

. . . .

4 WEDNESDAY

. . . .

5 THURSDAY

. . . .

◐♋♌ FRIDAY 6

○♌ SATURDAY 7

○♌♍ SUNDAY 8

THIS WEEK

There could be some unexpected twists and turns
to do with love and money this week, thanks to
an electric Venus—Uranus conjunction.

Super Full Moon in Virgo

Bring on the first Supermoon of 2020!

London	9 March	17:47
Sydney	10 March	04:47
Los Angeles	9 March	10:47
New York	9 March	13:47

Supermoons aren't as rare as you may think – we see up to six every year. They occur when a New or Full Moon closely coincides with perigee – the Moon's closest point to Earth in Her monthly orbit. They're more astronomical than astrological, but they're fun because a Super Full Moon will look up to 14 per cent larger and 30 per cent brighter than a Full Moon. Plus, the closer the Moon gets to Earth, the more we feel her powers, agreed?

This Full Moon is in the sign of Virgo, the Priestess, She of home and heart, She the unwed maiden. The word Virgo comes from the Latin 'unwed', so if you're unmarried, this is the time to celebrate it (even if you intend to change that status eventually). For everyone else, it's the right time to look at your life and see what's good and what's not. Virgo is traditionally the sign that's associated with women who literally sorted the wheat from the chaff, so do that with your life this Full Moon and be clear about what you need to release.

Note that Mercury retrograde also ends this week (on 10 March). That means the time to rethink, revisit and revise is coming to an end, and the time to take action on whatever you've been mulling over these past few weeks is approaching. It's also a powerful week for 'getting things done' and for meditation.

⚡ What This Lunation Means for You

Find your Rising sign in this list to discover which House the Moon is in for you (see page 16 for a quick guide): Aries – 6th House; Taurus – 5th House; Gemini – 4th House; Cancer – 3rd House; Leo – 2nd House; Virgo – 1st House; Libra – 12th House; Scorpio – 11th House; Sagittarius – 10th House; Capricorn – 9th House; Aquarius – 8th House; Pisces – 7th House.

⚡ Declutter Your Life

Wherever you are in the world, Full Moon in Virgo is a great time for decluttering. Whether you prefer a minimalist style or just want to be able to see the floor, use the meticulous energy of the Virgo Super Full Moon to let go of some stuff.

On a more esoteric note, there's a strong Divine Feminine energy around this week, so if you like to connect with the Goddesses, this is the time to call in Virgo Goddess Vesta. In Roman times she was the keeper of hearth, home, family and vestal virgins. To connect with Vesta's energy, place an image of her on your altar before you meditate.

Full Moon Forgiveness List

Full Moon is an important time for forgiveness, to practise gratitude and to release negativity. What do you need to let go of this month? Who do you need to forgive? What or whom do you need to practise gratitude for?

Visit moonmessages.com/diarymeditations to listen to the Moon meditation for this month, ideally before you make your list below. This will enable you to write from the heart.

_____

_____

_____

_____

_____

_____

_____

_____

_____

_____

⚵ Questions to Ask at This Full Moon

Is my home too cluttered? If so, where do I most need to declutter?

_____

_____

_____

_____

How could I be more helpful to others?

_____

_____

_____

_____

Do I nit-pick at others? In which areas of my life do I need to let go of doing this?

_____

_____

_____

_____

MARCH WEEK 11

. . . .

9 MONDAY

Super Full Moon
London   17:47
Los Angeles 10:47
New York   13:47

. . . .

10 TUESDAY

Super Full Moon
Sydney   04:47

Mercury retrograde ends.
. . . .

11 WEDNESDAY

♎︎○

. . . .

12 THURSDAY

♎︎♏︎↗○

. . . .

◗ ♏︎

FRIDAY 13

◖ ♏︎ ♐︎

SATURDAY 14

◖ ♐︎

SUNDAY 15

THIS WEEK

We're now in the waning cycle of the Moon which is the time to allow things to fall away. Think of it as a time just to accept and be. Mercury retrograde ends on Tuesday.

MARCH WEEK 12

....

16 MONDAY

What are you grateful for right now?
....

17 TUESDAY

....

18 WEDNESDAY

....

19 THURSDAY

....

 FRIDAY 20

Spring Equinox/Ostara (UK/USA); Autumn Equinox/Mabon (Aus)

 SATURDAY 21

♓ SUNDAY 22

THIS WEEK

This week brings Ostara, also known as the Spring Equinox,
in the northern hemisphere. In the southern hemisphere it's the
Autumn Equinox. Either way, it's a time to come into balance.

New Moon in Aries

The start of a new astrological year and time to take action.

London	24 March	09:28
Sydney	24 March	20:28
Los Angeles	24 March	02:28
New York	24 March	05:28

So, here we are at the New Moon in Aries. This occurs just once in 2020 and it's the moment of the year to recommit to anything that matters to you. It's more or less a restart time, the astrological new year and, in 2020, it's also important as it takes in the energy building between the two mighty planets Jupiter and Pluto. Sometimes we mere mortals need to make massive changes in our lives, and it could be argued that those changes should start here!

If you want to use the Aries energy to manifest, commit now to manifesting courage both for yourself and the people you love. Aries is all about the courage to chase our dreams, so ask yourself the classic question: What would you do if you knew you couldn't fail? Answer that question now!

This is a kind of second new year and the start of the new astrological year because Aries is, of course, the first of the

12 signs of the zodiac. The movement of the Sun into Aries heralds the start of spring in the northern hemisphere and autumn in the southern hemisphere. If you made new year resolutions you've since forgotten about, this is the week to get back on track. Also be sure to make some wishes and use the power of the New Moon in Aries to make 2020 the year you want it to be!

✵ What This Lunation Means for You

Find your Rising sign in this list to discover which House the Moon is in for you (see page 16 for a quick guide): Aries – 1st House; Taurus – 12th House; Gemini – 11th House; Cancer – 10th House; Leo – 9th House; Virgo – 8th House; Libra – 7th House; Scorpio – 6th House; Sagittarius – 5th House; Capricorn – 4th House; Aquarius – 3rd House; Pisces – 2nd House.

✵ A Fire Ritual

Because Aries energy is fiery, working with fire can be really effective at this time. One ceremony I perform is a simple fire ritual:

1. Place a fireproof dish on a level surface in a safe location.

2. Add some paper and kindling, and set fire to them.

3. Stare into the flames and invoke the Goddess Athena and the Archangel Ariel who work with the Aries energy.

4. Ask them for any help you need.

5. Set some really solid intentions for the year ahead – it's a super-powerful time to do this!

New Moon Wishes and Intentions

What are you manifesting this New Moon? Before you make your list of dreams and desires, visit moonmessages.com/diarymeditations and listen to the Moon meditation for this month. This will enable you to think from the heart – the best place to be. Then go through your list and 'feel' each wish as real, or feel the feeling of it being fulfilled.

_____

_____

_____

_____

_____

_____

_____

_____

_____

_____

_____

⚸ Questions to Ask at This New Moon

What is my #1 goal for the year ahead?

_____

_____

_____

_____

Do I need to be (a) less aggressive or (b) more assertive, and in which areas of my life?

_____

_____

_____

_____

What can I do to focus on myself this month?

_____

_____

_____

_____

_____

MARCH WEEK 13

....

23 MONDAY

....

24 TUESDAY

New Moon
London   09:28
Sydney   20:28
Los Angeles 02:28
New York   05:28

....

25 WEDNESDAY

....

26 THURSDAY

....

 FRIDAY 27

 SATURDAY 28

○♉♊ SUNDAY 29

THIS WEEK

It's a big week astrologically as the planet of hard work and hard times, Saturn, finally moves out of Capricorn into Aquarius after a two-year stay.

April

This month brings one of the biggest astrology headlines of the year: Jupiter meets Pluto in the skies. This is a major, potentially life-changing alignment which only happens about once every 12 years (this is how long it takes Jupiter to move through all 12 signs of the zodiac).

It makes now a time to ask yourself what massive changes do you need to make in your life, to open yourself up to positive transformation? Incorporate your answers into your Full Moon and New Moon work. Release what's

Super Full Moon in Libra		
London	8 April	03:35
Sydney	8 April	12:35
Los Angeles	7 April	19:35
New York	7 April	22:35
New Moon in Taurus		
London	23 April	03:25
Sydney	23 April	12:25
Los Angeles	22 April	19:25
New York	22 April	22:25

blocking you from making these changes at Full Moon and set your intentions about them at New Moon. Job done!

Also remember to think about what you're grateful for in your life and decide on your biggest aim for the month.

M	T	W	T	F	S	S
		1 ◐	2	3	4	5
6	7	8 ○	9	10	11	12
13	14 ◐	15	16	17	18	19
20	21	22	23 ●	24	25	26
27	28	29	30 ◐			

～ Things to do this month ～

1. Believe that huge change is possible for you.
2. Set some New Moon intentions around finance, property and possessions.
3. Avoid unpleasant people whenever possible and especially at the end of this month.

MAR/APR WEEK 14

....

30 MONDAY

....

31 TUESDAY

....

1 WEDNESDAY

What are you grateful for right now?
....

2 THURSDAY

....

 ☉ ♌

FRIDAY 3

☉ ♌ ♍

SATURDAY 4

☉ ♍

SUNDAY 5

THIS WEEK

Sunday brings a super-powerful Jupiter–Pluto link that reminds us that change is possible. Better yet, it's taking place in the waxing cycle, so is extra powerful!

Super Full Moon in Libra

A great time to make up… or break up.

London	8 April	03:35
Sydney	8 April	12:35
Los Angeles	7 April	19:35
New York	7 April	22:35

We're now in what you might call very 'high energetic times'. We've just had a massive planetary alignment in the form of Jupiter and Pluto, one of the astrological highlights of the year, and we'll still be feeling the effects this week. Plus, we have the Full Moon in Libra.

In a nutshell, the cosmic portals are now wide open for massive (Jupiter) transformations (Pluto) and especially important relationships (Libra).

So think about your most important one-to-one relationships and be honest about where they're going right and wrong. What do you no longer wish to put up with? Does one of these relationships involve drama that you're ready to move on from? If so, the time to work on this is between now and the end of June when this Jupiter–Pluto aspect repeats.

Of course, there could also be resentments you need to release – again, this is the time to do so. Forgiveness is the quickest way to clear the karma between you and someone else, and I've included a simple ceremony below.

⚳ What This Lunation Means for You

Find your Rising sign in this list to discover which House the Moon is in for you (see page 16 for a quick guide): Aries – 7th House; Taurus – 6th House; Gemini – 5th House; Cancer – 4th House; Leo – 3rd House; Virgo – 2nd House; Libra – 1st House; Scorpio – 12th House; Sagittarius – 11th House; Capricorn – 10th House; Aquarius – 9th House; Pisces – 8th House.

⚳ A Simple Forgiveness Ceremony

You can perform this ceremony at any Full Moon, but it will be extra powerful this week:

1. Take some deep, cleansing breaths.

2. Now think of anyone who has upset you. List their name(s) and what they did to upset you on a sheet of paper. Go back to your childhood if necessary, to anyone who, seemingly, did you wrong and whom you haven't yet forgiven.

3. Close your eyes and, in turn, visualize each person inside a pink bubble (pink is one of the colours of love), smiling at you. Create a good feeling between the two of you.

4. Say silently or out loud: 'I forgive you,' and then let them float off in their bubble.

Full Moon Forgiveness List

Full Moon is an important time for forgiveness, to practise gratitude and to release negativity. What do you need to let go of this month? Who do you need to forgive? What or whom do you need to practise gratitude for?

Visit moonmessages.com/diarymeditations to listen to the Moon meditation for this month, ideally before you make your list below. This will enable you to write from the heart.

_____

_____

_____

_____

_____

_____

_____

_____

_____

_____

⚳ Questions to Ask at This Full Moon

Who do I most need to forgive (apart from myself!) for any perceived failures or upsets?

_____

_____

_____

_____

In which relationship(s) am I going to try hard to find a balance?

_____

_____

_____

_____

Where in my life have I been thinking too much about others' needs and ignoring my own?

_____

_____

_____

_____

APRIL   WEEK 15

....

6 MONDAY

♍︎♎︎

....

7 TUESDAY

♎︎○

Full Moon
Los Angeles   19:35
New York   22:35

....

8 WEDNESDAY

♎︎♏︎○

Full Moon
London   03:35
Sydney   12:35

....

9 THURSDAY

♏︎○

....

○ m♐♐ FRIDAY 10

○ ♐ SATURDAY 11

◐ ♐ SUNDAY 12

THIS WEEK

*The Full Moon in Libra is a time to get back in balance
with what you give and what you receive. It's also time for
a vanity check and to rein it in if it's out of control!*

APRIL WEEK 16

13 MONDAY

14 TUESDAY

What are you grateful for right now?

15 WEDNESDAY

16 THURSDAY

 ♒ ♓   FRIDAY 17

 ♓   SATURDAY 18

 ♓   SUNDAY 19

THIS WEEK

Don't let your ego get in your way this week.
The Sun, which represents ego, clashes with, in this
order, obsessive Pluto and over-the-top Jupiter.

New Moon in Taurus

If there's a time to manifest money, this is it!

London	23 April	03:25
Sydney	23 April	12:25
Los Angeles	22 April	19:25
New York	22 April	22:25

With clashes between the Sun and Saturn, and Mercury and Pluto this New Moon in Taurus week, it's time for everyone to work through their blocks to abundance. If you're sorted financially, thank your lucky stars and help someone else!

The thing to understand is that money is energy. It really is. Think about it: money is printed on paper (or 'encoded' in plastic) and we decide that a £10 note or a $20 bill mean something. It's just paper. Or we go cashless, and a little plastic card and a computer calculate how 'much' we have. Both forms are just energy that we exchange for services.

So, depending on where we are in our consciousness around money, the more or less we think we deserve is exactly what we'll attract. The more you think you deserve the more you'll attract, and if you think of money as somehow dirty or the root of evil, the less you'll attract. If you can get your head around this idea, you'll start to realize there's nothing at all wrong with creating wealth in your life for yourself, and for your family and friends. Remember, we're here to learn how to create, and creating financial abundance and all the creature comforts that buys is a fine thing! Just remember to be generous too. That's a key to working with the exchangeable energy of money.

⚵ What This Lunation Means for You

Find your Rising sign in this list to discover which House the Moon is in for you (see page 16 for a quick guide): Aries – 2nd House; Taurus – 1st House; Gemini – 12th House; Cancer – 11th House; Leo – 10th House; Virgo – 9th House; Libra – 8th House; Scorpio – 7th House; Sagittarius – 6th House; Capricorn – 5th House; Aquarius – 4th House; Pisces – 3rd House.

⚵ Affirmations for Abundance

At this lunation I'd like to draw on the wisdom of three of my favourite abundance coaches. Repeat one, two or all of these affirmations in the days ahead and watch as you start to create more wealth:

'I have a perfect work in a perfect way;
I give perfect service for perfect pay.'
FLORENCE SCOVEL SHINN

'I serve, I deserve.'
DENISE DUFFIELD-THOMAS

'I make a lot of money and I help a lot of people!'
T. HARV EKER

New Moon Wishes and Intentions

What are you manifesting this New Moon? Before you make your list of dreams and desires, visit moonmessages.com/diarymeditations and listen to the Moon meditation for this month. This will enable you to think from the heart – the best place to be. Then go through your list and 'feel' each wish as real, or feel the feeling of it being fulfilled.

_____

_____

_____

_____

_____

_____

_____

_____

_____

_____

_____

_____

_____

⚷ Questions to Ask at This New Moon

Do I believe I deserve more cash, and if so, am I willing to take inspired action to create it?

_____

_____

_____

_____

What do I need to manifest to feel more comfortable?

_____

_____

_____

_____

Am I tapping into sensuality as much as I would like to? If not, how can I make sure I do this more often?

_____

_____

_____

_____

APRIL WEEK 17

....

20 MONDAY

....

21 TUESDAY

....

22 WEDNESDAY

New Moon
Los Angeles   19:25
New York   22:25

....

23 THURSDAY

New Moon
London   03:25
Sydney   12:25

....

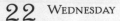

FRIDAY 24

SATURDAY 25

SUNDAY 26

THIS WEEK

On Friday we enter the waxing cycle, moving from New Moon to Full Moon, so start thinking about what you want to manifest in the month ahead.

May

This month brings Venus retrograde, which happens about once every 18 months (as opposed to, for example, Mercury retrograde, which happens up to four times a year). It's a good time to step back and ask yourself what really matters to you.

This Venus retrograde is happening in the sign of Gemini, the sign of the New Moon this month. To work out how this affects your chart, see 'What this lunation means for you' on page 111. Whichever House the Moon is in for you is

Full Moon in Scorpio		
London	7 May	11:45
Sydney	7 May	20:45
Los Angeles	7 May	03:45
New York	7 May	06:45
New Moon in Gemini		
London	23 May	18:38
Sydney	23 May	03:38
Los Angeles	22 May	10:38
New York	22 May	13:38

where you should be weighing things up a bit. As usual, the beginning of the month is also the time to think about what you're grateful for and decide on your biggest aim for the weeks ahead.

M	T	W	T	F	S	S
				1	2	3
4	5	6	7 ○	8	9	10
11	12	13	14 ◐	15	16	17
18	19	20	21	22 ●	23	24
25	26	27	28	29	30 ◑	31

~ Things to do this month ~

1. Write a list of your top five priorities.
2. Plan your life according to these priorities.
3. Give a friend or your partner space if they need it.

APRIL WEEK 18

27 MONDAY

28 TUESDAY

29 WEDNESDAY

30 THURSDAY

What are you grateful for right now?

 FRIDAY 1

Festivals of Beltane (UK/USA) and Samhain (Aus)

SATURDAY 2

SUNDAY 3

THIS WEEK

*Taurus energy is very sensual – tap into it this week
as Beltane is celebrated in the northern hemisphere
and Samhain is celebrated Down Under.*

Full Moon in Scorpio

Let go of self-criticism.

London	7 May	11:45
Sydney	7 May	20:45
Los Angeles	7 May	03:45
New York	7 May	06:45

The key this Full Moon week is communication. That's because by far the most active planet is Mercury, also known as the planet of communications.

Scorpio is the sign with the sting in its tail, so take time this week to think about whether you've been a little too stinging in your communications with someone. Scorpio is also the sign that holds a grudge. Add that to the intense Mercury action this week and it could be time for you to release (Full Moon) a grudge (Scorpio). Every Full Moon offers the chance to forgive, move on and detox your emotions, but if you've fallen out with someone and want to make up, the scene is truly set with this week's Full Moon in Scorpio.

Scorpio Moons can be super intense, but this year the Full Moon is harmonizing with Neptune which should soften the edges a little and provide a more mystical quality. So be sure to tap in and take advantage!

☿ What This Lunation Means for You

Find your Rising sign in this list to discover which House the Moon is in for you (see page 16 for a quick guide): Aries – 8th House; Taurus – 7th House; Gemini – 6th House; Cancer – 5th House; Leo – 4th House; Virgo – 3rd House; Libra – 2nd House; Scorpio – 1st House; Sagittarius – 12th House; Capricorn – 11th House; Aquarius – 10th House; Pisces – 9th House.

☿ Release Anger on Your Path to Inner Peace

Most of us have at least one person in our life who we're upset with. It could be someone who gave us a hard time at school, at work, last week, last year or a decade ago. This particular Scorpio Full Moon has all the elements needed to work on releasing this anger that, in the end, only holds us back. Follow this simple exercise to make it happen:

1. Think about who you need to forgive.

2. Write down in detail what happened and why you were upset. This might seem like focusing on the negative, but often, once you start writing, you realize that it doesn't matter to you as much as it once did.

3. Once you've finished writing, burn the sheet of paper.

4. Visit YouTube and listen to the wonderful meditation 'Ganesh Maha Mantra to Remove All Obstacles', which will help to clear your path to inner peace.

Full Moon Forgiveness List

Full Moon is an important time for forgiveness, to practise gratitude and to release negativity. What do you need to let go of this month? Who do you need to forgive? What or whom do you need to practise gratitude for?

Visit moonmessages.com/diarymeditations to listen to the Moon meditation for this month, ideally before you make your list below. This will enable you to write from the heart.

_____

_____

_____

_____

_____

_____

_____

_____

_____

_____

⚵ Questions to Ask at This Full Moon

How's my sex life? Does it need some TLC?

_____

_____

_____

_____

Have I been mean? What can I do to make amends?

_____

_____

_____

_____

What deep feelings do I need to process?

_____

_____

_____

_____

_____

MAY WEEK 19

....

4 MONDAY   ♍︎♎︎○

....

5 TUESDAY   ♎︎○

....

6 WEDNESDAY   ♎︎♏︎○

....

7 THURSDAY   ♏︎○

Full Moon
London   11:45
Sydney   20:45
Los Angeles 03:45
New York   06:45

....

◯ ♏⟩♐   FRIDAY **8**

◯ ♐   SATURDAY **9**

◯ ♐♑   SUNDAY **10**

THIS WEEK

*Many people want magic to happen
with no effort. It doesn't work like that.
You have to believe in your own magic!*

MAY WEEK 20

....

11 MONDAY ♑ ☽

....

12 TUESDAY ♑ ♒ ☽

....

13 WEDNESDAY ♒ ☽

....

Venus goes retrograde (until 25 June).

14 THURSDAY ♒ ◑

....

What are you grateful for right now?

....

 FRIDAY **15**

☽♓ SATURDAY **16**

☽♓♈ SUNDAY **17**

THIS WEEK

If you have an upset at the start of the week, don't panic.
You should be able to sort things out by the end of it.

New Moon in Gemini

Remember not to talk in riddles.

London	22 May	18:38
Sydney	23 May	03:38
Los Angeles	22 May	10:38
New York	22 May	13:38

This week's New Moon in Gemini brings *the* time of the year to manifest better communications. It also brings a potentially confusing Mercury/Venus/Neptune clash which pretty much assures us that some things are going to be as clear as mud! We can also expect confusion in love, about money and pretty much everything else! So what to do?

1. Understand that sometimes life is just confusing and there's nothing we can do about it.

2. Believe that at these times we need to keep the faith that all shall be well.

3. Remember that life is constantly unfolding, and even if you're not sure what's coming next, you soon will be.

4. Meditate, meditate, meditate. At the very least, it will calm a troubled mind.

5. Speak your truth. If you're honest, you're halfway there.

During this week, remember that the words we say create our lives and they have incredible power. At this New Moon in Gemini, it should be obvious where you have room for improvement in terms of how well (or not!) you're getting your message across to those you most want to hear it.

⚶ What This Lunation Means for You

Find your Rising sign in this list to discover which House the Moon is in for you (see page 16 for a quick guide): Aries – 3rd House; Taurus – 2nd House; Gemini – 1st House; Cancer – 12th House; Leo – 11th House; Virgo – 10th House; Libra – 9th House; Scorpio – 8th House; Sagittarius – 7th House; Capricorn – 6th House; Aquarius – 5th House; Pisces – 4th House.

⚶ A Ritual to Call in the Goddess Saraswati

If you like to work with Goddess energy, call on Saraswati to help improve your communication skills:

1. On the night of the New Moon (or as soon as you can afterwards) create a ritual space by tidying, burning some essential oil (bergamot is very good), lowering the lights and lighting a beeswax (pollution-free) candle.

2. Repeat this chant to Saraswati: *'May Saraswati, the Goddess of sound and speech, enlighten us all!'*

3. Make a list of three people you need better communication with and send them love. Meditate on your intention to communicate better with them and everyone.

New Moon Wishes and Intentions

What are you manifesting this New Moon? Before you make your list of dreams and desires, visit moonmessages.com/diarymeditations and listen to the Moon meditation for this month. This will enable you to think from the heart – the best place to be. Then go through your list and 'feel' each wish as real, or feel the feeling of it being fulfilled.

_____

_____

_____

_____

_____

_____

_____

_____

_____

_____

_____

_____

⚇ Questions to Ask at This New Moon

Have I been getting my message across, and if not, what can I do about it?

_____

_____

_____

_____

Have I been as honest with myself and others as I could be? Ask 'Is it true, kind or necessary?' before answering.

_____

_____

_____

_____

Do I need to do some more flirting? Gemini is a super-flirty energy and flirting does the spirit _good_!

_____

_____

_____

_____

MAY WEEK 21

....

18 MONDAY

....

19 TUESDAY

....

20 WEDNESDAY

....

21 THURSDAY

....

FRIDAY 22

New Moon
London   18:38
Los Angeles 10:38
New York   13:38

SATURDAY 23

New Moon
Sydney   03:38

SUNDAY 24

THIS WEEK

*The Gemini Archangel is Zadkiel, who can help with tactful
communication. Ask for his help with this chant: 'Dearest Archangel
Zadkiel, please be with me as I express myself openly and honestly. Help me
to reach my full potential when it comes to communicating. Thank you.'*

MAY WEEK 22

25 MONDAY

26 TUESDAY

27 WEDNESDAY

28 THURSDAY

 Friday 29

 Saturday 30

What are you grateful for right now?

 Sunday 31

This Week

*There aren't many planetary alignments this week,
but the Mars–Uranus alignment brings all the
energy you need. Use it by keeping busy!*

June

June brings the second of three eclipse seasons this year (following the first in December–January with a third to follow in November-December). An eclipse season is a period of several weeks during which all the lunations are eclipses. They act like energetic portals inviting us to step through into a new life. The current eclipse season lasts until the 5 July Full Moon eclipse in Capricorn.

This month also brings a hugely important and potentially transformational Jupiter–Pluto conjunction,

Full Moon eclipse in Sagittarius		
London	5 June	20:12
Sydney	6 June	05:12
Los Angeles	5 June	12:12
New York	5 June	15:12
New Moon eclipse in Cancer		
London	21 June	07:41
Sydney	21 June	16:41
Los Angeles	20 June	23:41
New York	21 June	02:41

which means it's a super-important time to ditch the past and take inspired action to create your future.

Remember to think about what you're grateful for and decide on your biggest aim for the month ahead.

M	T	W	T	F	S	S
1	2	3	4	5 ○	6	7
8	9	10	11	12	13 ◐	14
15	16	17	18	19	20	21 ●
22	23	24	25	26	27	28 ◑
29	30					

~ *Things to do this month* ~

1. Make sure you work with the Full and the New Moon – they're super-charged!

2. Practise radical forgiveness of yourself and others.

3. Get really clear about what you want – your wishes will be extra powerful at the time of an eclipse!

Full Moon Eclipse in Sagittarius

It's eclipse season and the time to change gear!

London	5 June	20:12
Sydney	6 June	05:12
Los Angeles	5 June	12:12
New York	5 June	15:12

Once you start to work with the Moon, you'll feel how much more intense the energies of an eclipse season can be. I can clearly recall my first eclipse as an astrologer – I was so aware of it. It was in my Star sign at the same time Saturn was trolling over my Venus and I was going through a horrible break-up. You don't forget something like that. It was intense. The Universe changes gears during an eclipse and my life changed gears at that time. I'd been hanging on to the relationship, even though I knew it was toxic, and the eclipse loosened my grip and put me on my right path. That's what they do. The more 'off path' you are, the more unceremoniously you'll be put back on the path your soul wants to be on, nay, *came* here to be on.

So, this week think about what in your life you know you need to release but are still hanging on to for all the wrong reasons. And if there's nothing like that in your life, look around for a friend or family member who's going through a tough time. If it happens to be your birthday or half-birthday this week, you'll feel the eclipse intensely! You'll also feel it strongly if you're Sagittarius or Sagittarius Rising (as the eclipse is in Sagittarius). Embrace it!

⚛ What This Lunation Means for You

Find your Rising sign in this list to discover which House the Moon is in for you (see page 16 for a quick guide): Aries – 9th House; Taurus – 8th House; Gemini – 7th House; Cancer – 6th House; Leo – 5th House; Virgo – 4th House; Libra – 3rd House; Scorpio – 2nd House; Sagittarius – 1st House; Capricorn – 12th House; Aquarius – 11th House; Pisces – 10th House.

⚛ Goddess Athena and Archangel Michael

I look forward to eclipses with cautious anticipation. If you're living in alignment with your own values, there's a good chance nothing too dramatic will happen; perhaps just an adjustment, if you need one. One way to work with the eclipse energy is to ask the Goddess Athena and/or Archangel Michael, both of whom have mighty swords, to cut your ties with the past. There really is nothing more important to do at the time of a Full Moon eclipse, no matter which sign it's in. Visualize the etheric cords between you and others dropping away. Relax, if someone is good for you, they'll come back even after this exercise. Think of it as a freshening up of your energies.

Full Moon Forgiveness List

Full Moon is an important time for forgiveness, to practise gratitude and to release negativity. What do you need to let go of this month? Who do you need to forgive? What or whom do you need to practise gratitude for?

Visit moonmessages.com/diarymeditations to listen to the Moon meditation for this month, ideally before you make your list below. This will enable you to write from the heart.

_____

_____

_____

_____

_____

_____

_____

_____

_____

_____

⚹ Questions to Ask at This Full Moon

Have I been carefree to the point of being careless? If so, when?

_____

_____

_____

_____

How can I make sure I see the bigger picture of life?

_____

_____

_____

_____

Have I been preachy? Detail any occasions.

_____

_____

_____

_____

JUNE WEEK 23

1 MONDAY ♎ ◑

2 TUESDAY ♎ ♏ ◑

3 WEDNESDAY ♏ ◑

4 THURSDAY ♏ ♐ ◑

◯ ♐   FRIDAY 5

Full Moon eclipse
London   20:12
Los Angeles 12:12
New York   15:12

◯ ♐♑   SATURDAY 6

Full Moon eclipse
Sydney   05:12

◯ ♑   SUNDAY 7

THIS WEEK

*The planet of love, Venus, is retrograde as the eclipse takes
place, so for some there's going to be a walk down memory
lane – maybe for reconciliation, maybe for closure.*

JUNE WEEK 24

....

8 MONDAY ♑ ◗

....

9 TUESDAY ♑ ♒ ◗

....

10 WEDNESDAY ♒ ◗

....

11 THURSDAY ♒ ♓ ◗

....

 FRIDAY 12

 SATURDAY 13

What are you grateful for right now?

● ♈ SUNDAY 14

THIS WEEK

*We're now smack-bang in the middle of eclipse
season, so expect the energies to feel pretty intense
and remember to focus on the positive.*

New Moon Eclipse in Cancer

Get with the programme – you're a powerful being!

London	21 June	07:41
Sydney	21 June	16:41
Los Angeles	20 June	23:41
New York	21 June	02:41

This New Moon eclipse is a powerful one. It's on the critical degree, which is 0 degrees of any sign, so it's the start of a new cycle. It's also taking place under the approaching Jupiter–Pluto conjunction, which happens only once every 12 years or so, excluding retrogrades. For ephemeris eagles, the Jupiter–Pluto connection will peak in November, so whatever you put your energy into now should start to show signs of manifestation later this year.

The more I think and write about working with the Moon, the clearer I am that it really works. I don't think I've figured out the secret code of the Universe; however, I do believe that Moonology and astrology provide a key to tracking and working with universal energy. I'm not saying that we can create every single thing we want by using the methods I include in this diary, but I really believe that our intentions and actions affect our future, as does the way our minds perceive the world. So if you want to test the degree to which you're creating your own reality, consciously or unconsciously, hook into the energies of this New Moon eclipse and wish with love!

⚵ What This Lunation Means for You

Find your Rising sign in this list to discover which House the Moon is in for you (see page 16 for a quick guide): Aries – 4th House; Taurus – 3rd House; Gemini – 2nd House; Cancer – 1st House; Leo – 12th House; Virgo – 11th House; Libra – 10th House; Scorpio – 9th House; Sagittarius – 8th House; Capricorn – 7th House; Aquarius – 6th House; Pisces – 5th House.

⚵ A Special New Moon Wishing Ceremony

The energies are super-charged this week, so tune in to them with a special New Moon wishing ceremony. In addition to making your list of dreams and desires (see page 130) at the New Moon, ask the powerful Hindu Goddesses Saraswati, Lakshmi and Durga for help. Saraswati is the Goddess of wisdom and learning, so wish to be wise. Lakshmi is the Goddess of abundance and love, so wish for these things to flow into your life. Durga, the warrior Goddess, destroys ignorance, so invite her to set you straight!

The important thing to remember is that you need to wish with love and from the heart. Cancer is a water sign, so pick up on that element and tune in to your emotions. It shouldn't need saying, but you mustn't interfere with someone else's free will.

New Moon Wishes and Intentions

What are you manifesting this New Moon? Before you make your list of dreams and desires, visit moonmessages.com/diarymeditations and listen to the Moon meditation for this month. This will enable you to think from the heart – the best place to be. Then go through your list and 'feel' each wish as real, or feel the feeling of it being fulfilled.

_____

_____

_____

_____

_____

_____

_____

_____

_____

_____

_____

⚸ Questions to Ask at This New Moon

What do I want for myself and my loved ones? Do I believe it can happen? Remember to wish with love.

_____

_____

_____

_____

Describe how it is for the good of all (if not, watch out!).

_____

_____

_____

_____

Why do you think you deserve it? Remember that self-worth is crucial.

_____

_____

_____

_____

JUNE WEEK 25

15 MONDAY

16 TUESDAY

17 WEDNESDAY

18 THURSDAY

Mercury goes retrograde (until 12 July).

 FRIDAY 19

 SATURDAY 20

New Moon eclipse
Los Angeles   23:41

Summer Solstice/Litha (UK/USA)

SUNDAY 21

New Moon eclipse
London   07:41
Sydney   16:41
New York   02:41

Winter Solstice (Aus)

THIS WEEK

This week brings the Summer Solstice in the northern hemisphere and the Winter Solstice in the southern hemisphere. Happy solstice to you! Mercury goes retrograde on Thursday.

JUNE WEEK 26

....

22 MONDAY

....

23 TUESDAY

....

24 WEDNESDAY

....

25 THURSDAY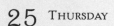

....

Venus retrograde ends.
....

 FRIDAY 26

♒︎♎ SATURDAY 27

☽♎ SUNDAY 28

What are you grateful for right now?

THIS WEEK

*We're still in eclipse season so the energy feels
emotionally intense right now. This time next
week the energies will have dissipated.*

July

This month begins with another eclipse – the third and final of this current eclipse season – which straddles the signs of Cancer and Capricorn. Cancer is always an emotional sign and Capricorn is currently the 'loaded' sign thanks to the powerful eclipse and planetary energies at work.

Make the most of these cosmic alignments by going really deep with your Full Moon release work. Meditate before you write your forgiveness list and then burn it. Feel all of your feelings; work through them and release them.

Full Moon eclipse in Capricorn		
London	5 July	05:44
Sydney	5 July	14:44
Los Angeles	4 July	21:44
New York	5 July	00:44
New Moon in Cancer		
London	20 July	18:32
Sydney	21 July	03:32
Los Angeles	20 July	10:32
New York	20 July	13:32

This month is also amazing for wishing, thanks to the Jupiter–Neptune connection. At the beginning of the month remember to practise gratitude and decide on your biggest aim for the coming weeks.

M	T	W	T	F	S	S
		1	2	3	4	5 ○
6	7	8	9	10	11	12
13 ◑	14	15	16	17	18	19
20 ●	21	22	23	24	25	26
27 ◐	28	29	30	31		

～ Things to do this month ～

1. Surrender everything to the Divine – again!

2. Understand you're getting a second chance with your New Moon wishes.

3. Tap into the amazing Jupiter–Neptune energies of 26 July with a meditation.

Full Moon Eclipse in Capricorn

Think of this as a time to turn a corner.

London	5 July	05:44
Sydney	5 July	14:44
Los Angeles	4 July	21:44
New York	5 July	00:44

This week brings a super-powerful eclipse, in Capricorn, the sign of Saturn, longevity, being sensible and adulthood, among other things. It comes in the aftermath of the powerful Jupiter–Pluto conjunction, so we have the makings of a big week.

The energies are high and if you're energy sensitive you'll feel them. This is a great time to meditate to help you stay in touch with your Higher Self (the part of you that knows you're connected to all life everywhere) and be guided on how best to use these energies. You're experiencing them for cosmic reasons, so *feel* all of your feelings and work with them. That's part of living consciously, and it's why working with the Moon... works! The lunar cycle helps to create magic.

This week also sees Saturn moving back into Capricorn after a brief foray into Aquarius. This marks the true beginning of the end of the Saturn-in-Capricorn phase, which has been active since December 2017. It's time to live consciously!

⚹ What This Lunation Means for You

Find your Rising sign in this list to discover which House the Moon is in for you (see page 16 for a quick guide): Aries – 10th House; Taurus – 9th House; Gemini – 8th House; Cancer – 7th House; Leo – 6th House; Virgo – 5th House; Libra – 4th House; Scorpio – 3rd House; Sagittarius – 2nd House; Capricorn – 1st House; Aquarius – 12th House; Pisces – 11th House.

⚹ Saturn, the True Cosmic Teacher

Just ahead of the Full Moon, think about what you've learned since December 2017 (when Saturn entered Capricorn). Bring in a ritualistic element of Earth to honour Capricorn; you could do this by surrounding yourself with crystals as you do this exercise. (If you don't have any crystals, now is the time to treat yourself to some!)

Ask how the lessons you've learned have shaped your life (or, dare I say, rocked your world!). These lessons are Saturn's gifts. They're not always easy to think about, but Saturn is a great cosmic teacher. Make a note of the most important thing you've learned and what, as a result, you now need to release under this Full Moon eclipse. Think about all areas of your life, from work to relationships, family and finances.

Full Moon Forgiveness List

Full Moon is an important time for forgiveness, to practise gratitude and to release negativity. What do you need to let go of this month? Who do you need to forgive? What or whom do you need to practise gratitude for?

Visit moonmessages.com/diarymeditations to listen to the Moon meditation for this month, ideally before you make your list below. This will enable you to write from the heart.

_____

_____

_____

_____

_____

_____

_____

_____

_____

_____

⨎ Questions to Ask at This Full Moon

Have I been ambitious to the point of ruthlessness?

_____

_____

_____

_____

When have I been obsessed with work to the detriment of my personal life?

_____

_____

_____

_____

Are there any times I've been hard-headed, hard-nosed or just too hard on others?

_____

_____

_____

_____

Jun/Jul Week 27

29 Monday
♎ ♏ ↗

30 Tuesday
♏ ↗ ☽

1 Wednesday
♏ ↗ ☽

2 Thursday
♏ ↗ ♐ ☽

○ ♐   FRIDAY 3

○ ♐♑   SATURDAY 4

Full Moon eclipse
Los Angeles   21:44

○ ♑   SUNDAY 5

Full Moon eclipse
London   05:44
Sydney   14:44
New York   00:44

THIS WEEK

*Sunday's Full Moon brings the Hindu festival of Guru
Purnima, a day to send thanks to your teachers.*

JULY WEEK 28

....

6 MONDAY   ♑ ♒ ○

....

7 TUESDAY   ♒ ○

....

8 WEDNESDAY   ♒ ♓ ◐

....

9 THURSDAY   ♓ ◐

....

◯♓   FRIDAY 10

◑♓♈   SATURDAY 11

◑♈   SUNDAY 12

Mercury retrograde ends.

THIS WEEK

We've now officially left the second eclipse season of the
year. Notice how quickly the intense energies even out again.
It's amazing! Mercury retrograde ends on Sunday.

July Week 29

---

13 Monday

What are you grateful for right now?

---

14 Tuesday

---

15 Wednesday

---

16 Thursday

FRIDAY 17

SATURDAY 18

SUNDAY 19

THIS WEEK

The Sun is clashing with excessive Jupiter and control-freak Pluto this week, so expect a few clashing egos to match the planets.

New Moon in Cancer

Shower the people you love with love...

London	20 July	18:32
Sydney	21 July	03:32
Los Angeles	20 July	10:32
New York	20 July	13:32

This week brings the second New Moon in Cancer of the year, so it's time to focus on family, hearth and home, if you haven't already been doing so. If you like to work with Goddesses, the energy this week is Diana. Hers is a very vibrant energy and isn't to be confused with the image of a Cancerian who likes to stay home and bake cookies! She's a woman who has earned her stripes. She takes in the maiden, the mother and the crone, but she's still a Cancerian through and through.

Soft and gentle Cancerian energy can be a bit clingy and insecure, so this week think about any parts of you about which you're insecure and send them love. Also think about family and the people you love, and send them love, too.

If you want to change your living situation, this is the time to visualize yourself in a new home. I strongly believe that we all end up in the homes that are right for us, so I wouldn't recommend visualizing a particular home. Instead, visualize yourself standing (solo or with loved ones) next to a 'Sold' or 'Let' sign, smiling and feeling delighted. Wish lovingly and say, 'This or something better now manifests for me under grace in perfect ways!'

☼ What This Lunation Means for You

Find your Rising sign in this list to discover which House the Moon is in for you (see page 16 for a quick guide): Aries – 4th House; Taurus – 3rd House; Gemini – 2nd House; Cancer – 1st House; Leo – 12th House; Virgo – 11th House; Libra – 10th House; Scorpio – 9th House; Sagittarius – 8th House; Capricorn – 7th House; Aquarius – 6th House; Pisces – 5th House.

☼ A Water Ceremony

With the New Moon in the water sign of Cancer, a water ceremony will work really well this week to help you manifest your wishes. Here's a simple yet magical one you can perform:

1. Pour yourself a glass of filtered water in a clean glass.

2. Write down your New Moon wishes.

3. Put your hands around the glass of water and recite your wishes into it, visualizing each one and *feeling* it as real (this is more important than anything else). As you speak, allow your breath to flow over the water.

4. Drink the water!

New Moon Wishes and Intentions

What are you manifesting this New Moon? Before you make your list of dreams and desires, visit moonmessages.com/diarymeditations and listen to the Moon meditation for this month. This will enable you to think from the heart – the best place to be. Then go through your list and 'feel' each wish as real, or feel the feeling of it being fulfilled.

_____

_____

_____

_____

_____

_____

_____

_____

_____

_____

_____

⚹ Questions to Ask at This New Moon

Have I been foolishly insecure, and if so, what can I do to make myself feel more secure?

_____

_____

_____

_____

Have I been giving my closest friends and family as much of my time and attention that they both need and deserve?

_____

_____

_____

_____

What do I want to create for myself in my private life in the coming year and how am I going to do that?

_____

_____

_____

_____

July Week 30

20 Monday

New Moon
London   18:32
Los Angeles 10:32
New York   13:32

21 Tuesday

New Moon
Sydney   03:32

22 Wednesday

23 Thursday

 ♍

FRIDAY 24

◖ ♍ ♎

SATURDAY 25

◐ ♎

SUNDAY 26

THIS WEEK

The cosmic vibes are strong this week, so tune in
through meditation, chanting or practising yoga.

July Week 31

27 Monday

What are you grateful for right now?

28 Tuesday

29 Wednesday

30 Thursday

🌑 ♐♑   FRIDAY 31

🌑 ♑   SATURDAY 1

Festivals of Lammas (UK/USA) and Imbolc (Aus)

🌑 ♑♒   SUNDAY 2

THIS WEEK

*Thanks to some intense Mercury action, this is a powerful week
for dreaming up ideas, talking things through, getting things
agreed upon and persuading people about your ideas.*

August

The first 10 days of August bring clashes between angry Mars, noisy Jupiter and furious Pluto, so if you sense your anger rising, it's a great time to double-down on your meditation, chanting or whatever you do to get into a Zen headspace. The first of the clashes takes place around the time of the Full Moon, bringing more intensity than you might like. The good news is that by the middle of the month, a series of harmonious alignments involving Mercury will offer you the space you need to talk things through and

Full Moon in Aquarius		
London	3 August	16:58
Sydney	4 August	01:58
Los Angeles	3 August	08:58
New York	3 August	11:58
New Moon in Leo		
London	19 August	03:41
Sydney	19 August	12:41
Los Angeles	18 August	19:41
New York	18 August	22:41

make peace. Note that this won't happen by itself – you'll need to make the most of the energies as they unfold!

As August begins, remember to think about what you're grateful for and decide on your biggest aim for the month.

M	T	W	T	F	S	S
					1	2
3 ○	4	5	6	7	8	9
10	11 ◖	12	13	14	15	16
17	18	19 ●	20	21	22	23
24	25 ◗	26	27	28	29	30
31						

⁓ Things to do this month ⁓

1. Use your energies extra wisely.
2. If you're striving to achieve something that just isn't possible, stop!
3. Invoke more self-confidence at the New Moon.

Full Moon in Aquarius

Think positive thoughts to attract positive experiences!

London	3 August	16:58
Sydney	4 August	01:58
Los Angeles	3 August	08:58
New York	3 August	11:58

As you know, every Full Moon is about letting go, but this Full Moon is perfect for letting go of an argument. This is because the most influential planetary link under this lunation is the opposition of Mercury, the communications planet, and Saturn, the planet of hard facts (and often difficulty). So if you've been having harsh words with someone, use this lunation to let it go. Life really is too short!

My magic formula in these situations is 'Feelings first, manifestation second'. Channeller Georgia Jean of circleevolution.com puts it a little more esoterically: 'Frequency first, manifestation second'. The message is that how we feel and the frequency we tune in to, such as joy, anger or fear, is what we manifest. So which frequency or feelings are you tuned in to?

As the Full Moon swells, your feelings are going to get stronger too, and in the process become easier to access. So if you know you're tuned in to negativity, then it's time to change. Reach for the best feeling you can about whatever is on your mind, and release as much negativity as you can this week. Forgive anyone who needs your forgiveness and declare that it's time to move on!

⁂ What This Lunation Means for You

Find your Rising sign in this list to discover which House the Moon is in for you (see page 16 for a quick guide): Aries – 11th House; Taurus – 10th House; Gemini – 9th House; Cancer – 8th House; Leo – 7th House; Virgo – 6th House; Libra – 5th House; Scorpio – 4th House; Sagittarius – 3rd House; Capricorn – 2nd House; Aquarius – 1st House; Pisces – 12th House.

⁂ The Goddess Isis Reclaimed

Tap into the power of the Full Moon in Aquarius with a meditation to Isis, Goddess of All Things, who will help with your release work. To invoke her, light a frankincense candle or put some frankincense oil in your diffuser, pour yourself a glass of grape juice or wine and say her name: 'Goddess Isis! You bring together the power of the Sun and Moon. What do I need to release?'

Sip your juice or wine and close your eyes to meditate. Just breathe. After a few minutes, take a pen and write down whatever comes to mind. Note that if you write anything that upsets you, chances are it's coming from your ego, because Isis is here to support you, not upset you.

Full Moon Forgiveness List

Full Moon is an important time for forgiveness, to practise gratitude and to release negativity. What do you need to let go of this month? Who do you need to forgive? What or whom do you need to practise gratitude for?

Visit moonmessages.com/diarymeditations to listen to the Moon meditation for this month, ideally before you make your list below. This will enable you to write from the heart.

_____

_____

_____

_____

_____

_____

_____

_____

_____

⚹ Questions to Ask at This Full Moon

Have I been living too much in my head and not enough in my heart? Make a note of when.

_____

_____

_____

_____

Are there any times in the last month when I tried to do things my way, just for the sake of it?

_____

_____

_____

_____

Whom have I tried hard to befriend, but for the wrong reasons?

_____

_____

_____

_____

AUGUST WEEK 32

3 MONDAY

Full Moon
London   16:58
Los Angeles 08:58
New York   11:58

4 TUESDAY

Full Moon
Sydney   01:58

5 WEDNESDAY

6 THURSDAY

☽⚹♈

FRIDAY 7

☽♈

SATURDAY 8

☽♈

SUNDAY 9

THIS WEEK

When the Full Moon is in Aquarius, it's the right time to ask yourself if you're doing what you're doing for other people or for yourself – and to find a balance.

AUGUST WEEK 33

10 MONDAY

11 TUESDAY

What are you grateful for right now?

12 WEDNESDAY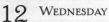

13 THURSDAY

 FRIDAY 14

SATURDAY 15

SUNDAY 16

THIS WEEK

This week brings a clash of titans – between angry Mars and furious Pluto – so expect intense emotions. You have been warned!

New Moon in Leo

It's a Black Moon and a chance to celebrate life!

London	19 August	03:41
Sydney	19 August	12:41
Los Angeles	18 August	19:41
New York	18 August	22:41

This week's New Moon in Leo is also known as a Black Moon – the third New Moon in a season (summer in the northern hemisphere; winter in the southern hemisphere) with four New Moons instead of three. This only happens about once every 33 months. The additional New Moon offers us more chances to manifest our dreams and desires, so what are you waiting for? Have you been keeping up with your wishing practices? You might already have everything you want in your life, but if not and you really want something, this is the time to use the power of the New Moon to make your wishes and set your intentions.

Another non-astrological but auspicious overlay to this New Moon is that, in India, it marks the festival of Ganesh Chaturthi, which celebrates the birth of the revered Hindu God, Ganesha. If you're not familiar with this amazing other-worldly being with an elephant's head, then use this New Moon to get acquainted. Ask Ganesha for help whenever you need to overcome any obstacles or are starting something new – and, of course, the New Moon is all about new beginnings.

The energies of this New Moon are very much about expressing ourselves creatively. So what do you want to say to someone, or to the world? Ask Ganesha to help you!

✳ What This Lunation Means for You

Find your Rising sign in this list to discover which House the Moon is in for you (see page 16 for a quick guide): Aries – 5th House; Taurus – 4th House; Gemini – 3rd House; Cancer – 2nd House; Leo – 1st House; Virgo – 12th House; Libra – 11th House; Scorpio – 10th House; Sagittarius – 9th House; Capricorn – 8th House; Aquarius – 7th House; Pisces – 6th House.

✳ A Chant for Ganesha

Ganesha is one of my favourite energies. Try the following chant to connect with him:

'Glowing like the colour of the Moon, Ganesha helps me
I meditate upon Ganesha's ever-smiling face
Remover of obstacles in my path
Ganesha guide me at New Moon!'

I've also recorded this chant, which you can download at moonmessages.com/diary2020. I hope it will help you to visualize what you want for yourself.

New Moon Wishes and Intentions

What are you manifesting this New Moon? Before you make your list of dreams and desires, visit moonmessages.com/diarymeditations and listen to the Moon meditation for this month. This will enable you to think from the heart – the best place to be. Then go through your list and 'feel' each wish as real, or feel the feeling of it being fulfilled.

✵ Questions to Ask at This New Moon

Am I showing the world what I have to offer, and if not, what am I going to do about it?

_____

_____

_____

_____

How can I work on my self-confidence?

_____

_____

_____

_____

Is there a creative project I need to recommit to? If so, am I willing to do it now?

_____

_____

_____

_____

AUGUST WEEK 34

....

17 MONDAY

....

18 TUESDAY

New Moon
Los Angeles   19:41
New York   22:41

....

19 WEDNESDAY

New Moon
London   03:41
Sydney   12:41

....

20 THURSDAY

....

 FRIDAY 21

 SATURDAY 22

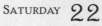 SUNDAY 23

THIS WEEK

The Leo New Moon is the ideal time to think about
where you need more confidence to succeed, and to commit
to lavishing yourself with more self-love!

AUGUST WEEK 35

....

24 MONDAY

....

25 TUESDAY ♏⚊♐

What are you grateful for right now?
....

26 WEDNESDAY ♐

....

27 THURSDAY ♐♑

....

WEEK 35 AUGUST

○ ♑   FRIDAY 28

○ ♑   SATURDAY 29

○ ♑ ♒   SUNDAY 30

THIS WEEK

*Wednesday is a day to tap into some great romance
vibes, so make it a date night if you're in love
and/or want to revitalize your relationship.*

September

This month we reach the end of the Full Moon cycle, since Pisces is the 12th and final sign of the zodiac. If you've worked with all of the Full Moons since the last Full Moon in Pisces (around this time last year), then pat yourself on the back. When you look back, can you see how far you've come? Can you see how working with forgiveness, release and surrender every month has helped you to clear blocks?

September sees the start of Mars retrograde, which happens only once every two or so years. It's a time when

Full Moon in Pisces		
London	2 September	06:22
Sydney	2 September	15:22
Los Angeles	1 September	22:22
New York	2 September	01:22
New Moon in Virgo		
London	17 September	12:00
Sydney	17 September	21:00
Los Angeles	17 September	04:00
New York	17 September	07:00

forging ahead becomes harder, so don't try too hard at this if you don't want to end up frustrated! At the beginning of the month, remember to think about what you're grateful for and decide on your biggest aim in the weeks ahead.

M	T	W	T	F	S	S
	1	2 ○	3	4	5	6
7	8	9	10 ◐	11	12	13
14	15	16	17 ●	18	19	20
21	22	23	24 ◑	25	26	27
28	29	30				

∼ Things to do this month ∼

1. Slow life down.
2. Take time to breathe.
3. Thank the Moon for Her guidance in the last year.

Full Moon in Pisces

The end of a Full Moon cycle and a time to reflect.

London	2 September	06:22
Sydney	2 September	15:22
Los Angeles	1 September	22:22
New York	2 September	01:22

This Full Moon in Pisces marks the end of the lunar cycle that began back in October 2019 with the Aries Full Moon. Why is this the end? As you know there are 12 zodiac signs, Aries being the first and Pisces being the last, so the Full Moon in Aries marks the start of a new cycle of 12 or 13 Full Moons over the course of 12 months, and the Full Moon in Pisces, which we have this week, is the last in the cycle.

What does this mean? For one thing, it's a time to reflect on the year since October 2019. How far have you come? The fact that it's September and not the beginning nor the end of the year shouldn't interfere in this process (though if you're in the northern hemisphere it's a little easier to see this period as an 'end' as it's the end of the summer). In particular, think about how well you've been balancing all that you need to do with your need for Zen time out and that Holy Grail, inner peace. If you need to bring more of one or the other into your life, this is the time to do so.

⚶ What This Lunation Means for You

Find your Rising sign in this list to discover which House the Moon is in for you (see page 16 for a quick guide): Aries – 12th House; Taurus – 11th House; Gemini – 10th House; Cancer – 9th House; Leo – 8th House; Virgo – 7th House; Libra – 6th House; Scorpio – 5th House; Sagittarius – 4th House; Capricorn – 3rd House; Aquarius – 2nd House; Pisces – 1st House.

⚶ Why You Should Let Go Now

Every Full Moon is a powerful time to let go and release, but this one is even more so. Here's why:

1. Pisces is the last sign of the zodiac, so when anything takes place in Pisces there's a sense that it's the final opportunity to do something before everything starts over. In this case, it's a wonderful time to release.

2. Pisces is a super-mystical and sacred sign (we all have Pisces in our chart somewhere), and the energy it creates is very conducive to doing sacred work, such as forgiving and letting go.

3. This year's Full Moon in Pisces is connecting with the Great Liberator planet Uranus, which means you really can break free of something that no longer serves you. What's it to be?

Full Moon Forgiveness List

Full Moon is an important time for forgiveness, to practise gratitude and to release negativity. What do you need to let go of this month? Who do you need to forgive? What or whom do you need to practise gratitude for?

Visit moonmessages.com/diarymeditations to listen to the Moon meditation for this month, ideally before you make your list below. This will enable you to write from the heart.

_____

_____

_____

_____

_____

_____

_____

_____

_____

⋇ Questions to Ask at This Full Moon

Have I been dreamy to the point of not getting enough done and making silly errors? If so, make a list.

_____

_____

_____

_____

Have I been meditating every day, and if not, why not?

_____

_____

_____

_____

Have I been in touch with my intuitive side, and following my dreams and hunches?

_____

_____

_____

_____

Aug/Sep Week 36

....

31 Monday

....

1 Tuesday

Full Moon
Los Angeles 22:22

....

2 Wednesday

Full Moon
London   06:22
Sydney   15:22
New York   01:22

....

3 Thursday

....

◯ ♈

FRIDAY 4

◯ ♈

SATURDAY 5

◯ ♈♉

SUNDAY 6

THIS WEEK

The planet of determination and drive, Mars, retrogrades this week. Slow things down and lower your expectations for getting things done speedily so you don't get frustrated at delays.

SEPTEMBER WEEK 37

7 MONDAY ♉

8 TUESDAY ♉♊

9 WEDNESDAY ♊

Mars goes retrograde (until 14 November).

10 THURSDAY ♊

What are you grateful for right now?

Friday 11

Saturday 12

Sunday 13

This Week

*It's a week to surrender all to the Divine as a sort of
insurance against manifesting something you later regret.*

New Moon in Virgo

It's time to get yourself together.

London	17 September	12:00
Sydney	17 September	21:00
Los Angeles	17 September	04:00
New York	17 September	07:00

This New Moon is perfect for getting more organized. If you're in the northern hemisphere, this timing works well as it coincides with back-to-school and work preparations. When better to go through all of your stuff and see what needs decluttering and tidying? And if you're in the southern hemisphere, you don't get off the hook! We might be just a few months out from the end of 2020, but summer beckons, so this is still an amazing time to commit to being healthier. Virgo has lots of other qualities too, including being on top of things, being of service to others and being healthy in a way that allows room for alternative methods and ideologies.

The energies of the week are rather intense, with planetary clashes between Venus (love) and Uranus (out of control), and Mercury (communication) and Jupiter (being over the top). If you feel like life is spinning beyond your comfort zone (and with this week's astrology it really might!), bringing the steady and reliable Virgo New Moon energy to bear will help. Think of it like the calm at the eye of a storm. Be the most Zen and organized person in any room you grace this week. And remember to b-r-e-a-t-h-e through the intensity.

⚹ What This Lunation Means for You

Find your Rising sign in this list to discover which House the Moon is in for you (see page 16 for a quick guide): Aries – 6th House; Taurus – 5th House; Gemini – 4th House; Cancer – 3rd House; Leo – 2nd House; Virgo – 1st House; Libra – 12th House; Scorpio – 11th House; Sagittarius – 10th House; Capricorn – 9th House; Aquarius – 8th House; Pisces – 7th House.

⚹ Make Lists for Success

Virgo is all about making lists, so start by writing down everything you need to do and what you want to do. Studies show that people perform better when they've done this. If you haven't tried it yet, this is the week to give it a go! I find paper lists are better because I can carry them around with me, whereas lists I make on a computer easily get lost.

Note that the Moon goes Void of Course (it doesn't make an aspect with any planet until it moves into the next sign of the zodiac) directly after the New Moon. It's said that whatever we start when the Moon is Void of Course will bear no fruit, so wait until She has moved into Libra (at least eight hours after the New Moon) to make your wishes.

New Moon Wishes and Intentions

What are you manifesting this New Moon? Before you make your list of dreams and desires, visit moonmessages.com/diarymeditations and listen to the Moon meditation for this month. This will enable you to think from the heart – the best place to be. Then go through your list and 'feel' each wish as real, or feel the feeling of it being fulfilled.

_____

_____

_____

_____

_____

_____

_____

_____

_____

_____

_____

☡ Questions to Ask at This New Moon

Being helpful to others creates good karma and in turn attracts good. Who do I commit to helping more this month?

_____

_____

_____

_____

Where in my life could I be healthier, and what is my plan to make that happen? Make a list!

_____

_____

_____

_____

Am I being too critical of myself or someone I care about?

_____

_____

_____

_____

SEPTEMBER WEEK 38

14 MONDAY

15 TUESDAY

16 WEDNESDAY

17 THURSDAY

New Moon
London   12:00
Sydney   21:00
Los Angeles 04:00
New York   07:00

 FRIDAY 18

 SATURDAY 19

 SUNDAY 20

THIS WEEK

At the beginning of the week the Moon is at the end of Her waning cycle, so go easy on yourself and don't take on too many commitments.

SEPTEMBER WEEK 39

---

21 MONDAY

---

22 TUESDAY

 Autumn Equinox/Mabon (UK/USA)

---

23 WEDNESDAY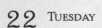

Spring Equinox/Ostara (Aus)

---

24 THURSDAY

What are you grateful for right now?

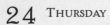

◑ ♑   FRIDAY 25

◑ ♑ ♒   SATURDAY 26

◑ ♒   SUNDAY 27

THIS WEEK

*Take a moment to honour the changing seasons. The northern hemisphere
sees the Autumn Equinox (Mabon), the mid-harvest festival, and in
the southern hemisphere it's the Spring Equinox (Ostara). At both
equinoxes, day and night are of approximately equal length.*

October

It's a month to dream big! October brings the last of the Jupiter–Neptune alignments for 2020. They've been about big dreams, massive manifestations and learning/teaching about spiritual topics. So tap in one more time, around 12 October, by making your vision board and practising creative visualization. Then reiterate your wishes a few days later at the time of the New Moon.

October brings not two but three lunations – two Full Moons and a New Moon – so the energy is likely to be

Full Moon in Aries		
London	1 October	22:05
Sydney	2 October	07:05
Los Angeles	1 October	14:05
New York	1 October	17:05
Super New Moon in Libra		
London	16 October	20:31
Sydney	17 October	06:31
Los Angeles	16 October	12:31
New York	16 October	15:31

emotionally charged. Go easy on yourself and the people you love, and remember to breathe through any drama.

Remember to think about what you're grateful for and decide on your biggest aim for the month ahead.

M	T	W	T	F	S	S
			1 ○	2	3	4
5	6	7	8	9	10 ◐	11
12	13	14	15	16 ●	17	18
19	20	21	22	23 ◑	24	25
26	27	28	29	30	31 ○	

～ Things to do this month ～

1. Declutter your home – the energies will really shift in your life.
2. Make a commitment about how you want your love life to progress.
3. Believe that your dreams can come true.

Full Moon in Aries

The start of the new lunar cycle and a time for healing.

London	1 October	22:05
Sydney	2 October	07:05
Los Angeles	1 October	14:05
New York	1 October	17:05

Aries is the first sign of the zodiac, so even though we're well into the second half of the year, the Full Moon in Aries marks the start of a new lunar cycle, so expect the energies to be extra high this week. If you've fallen off the bandwagon when it comes to working with the Full Moon, now is the time to recommit.

This week offers us two choices: healing or wounding. Healing comes because the Full Moon triggers Chiron, the healing planetoid. For some, this means that painful experiences will come to the surface for healing. Work with Chiron by asking yourself: 'What will healing look like to me?' 'How will I know that a particular hurt has been healed?' As ever, forgiveness will be a likely component. Whether this means forgiveness for yourself or someone else, it's almost always crucial if healing is to follow.

Soon after the Full Moon comes a face-off between the planet of communication, Mercury, and the planet of chaos that refuses to do as it's told, Uranus. So if you're upset with someone, take a breath and don't say too much too soon.

⚳ What This Lunation Means for You

Find your Rising sign in this list to discover which House the Moon is in for you (see page 16 for a quick guide): Aries – 1st House; Taurus – 12th House; Gemini – 11th House; Cancer – 10th House; Leo – 9th House; Virgo – 8th House; Libra – 7th House; Scorpio – 6th House; Sagittarius – 5th House; Capricorn – 4th House; Aquarius – 3rd House; Pisces – 2nd House.

⚳ Clearing Energy at the Full Moon

Here are some of my favourite energy-clearing methods to do at any Full Moon, but in particular this week:

1. Burn essential oils in your diffuser to transform the energy of a room in minutes. Good quality oils raise the vibration in amazing ways. If you're not into oils, burning incense has a similar effect.

2. Want an all-over-body experience? Oils in your bath or a salt bath using high-quality salts will cleanse you.

3. Meditation is great to cleanse your aura.

4. Burning medicinal herbs is great for cleansing air in the confined space of plant and human pathogenic bacteria. Rose petals, sandalwood powder, ghee, lotus seeds, turmeric and sage all work well.

Full Moon Forgiveness List

Full Moon is an important time for forgiveness, to practise gratitude and to release negativity. What do you need to let go of this month? Who do you need to forgive? What or whom do you need to practise gratitude for?

Visit moonmessages.com/diarymeditations to listen to the Moon meditation for this month, ideally before you make your list below. This will enable you to write from the heart.

_____

_____

_____

_____

_____

_____

_____

_____

_____

_____

⚹ Questions to Ask at This Full Moon

When have I been too quick to anger since the last Full Moon?

_____

_____

_____

_____

Do I need to breathe in more courage to do the things I want to do? How can I remember to do this?

_____

_____

_____

_____

Have I been too selfish or, contrariwise, too giving? When?

_____

_____

_____

_____

Sep/Oct Week 40

....

28 Monday ♒ ♓ ○

....

29 Tuesday ♓ ○

....

30 Wednesday ♓ ○

....

1 Thursday

Full Moon
London   22:05
Los Angeles 14:05
New York   17:05

....

○ ♈

Full Moon
Sydney   07:05

FRIDAY 2

○ ♊♉

SATURDAY 3

○ ♉

SUNDAY 4

THIS WEEK

There's a rather tense alignment between Mars and Saturn
this week, so watch out if you know you have problems
with authority and channel your energy wisely!

OCTOBER WEEK 41

....

5 MONDAY ♉🌖

....

6 TUESDAY ♉Ⅱ🌖

....

7 WEDNESDAY Ⅱ🌖

....

8 THURSDAY Ⅱ♋

....

 FRIDAY 9

 SATURDAY 10

What are you grateful for right now?

 SUNDAY 11

THIS WEEK

*Mars retrograde is clashing with Pluto this week,
so an old argument could come up – deal with it
properly and it should go away forever.*

Super New Moon in Libra

Time for a relationship reset.

London	16 October	20:31
Sydney	17 October	06:31
Los Angeles	16 October	12:31
New York	16 October	15:31

This is one of the stand-out weeks of the year, thanks to the Super New Moon in Libra, which is all about relationships, and the Jupiter–Neptune link, which is all about dreams and ideals. A Super New Moon occurs when the Moon is at Her closest point to Earth in Her monthly orbit.

The best way to tap into this energy is at the start of the week by making a list of the top five qualities you dream of attracting into your current or next relationship. This is something anyone can do, whether you're single and looking for love (in which case the list will be a pure wish list!), or already attached and want to think about how you'd like your relationship to evolve.

Lists such as this are most often recommended for people who want to attract love into their life, rather than for those already in a relationship. In fact, they work equally well for both groups, as those already in a cherished relationship often want to work on making things better. We live in such a disposable society and sometimes relationships are viewed as disposable, too. Remember, though, that relationships often teach us more about ourselves than anything else. So it's just as important to nurture the love you have with good intention, as it can also help to draw in new love when you're single.

The Moon goes Void of Course after the New Moon, so make your wishes at least 12 hours after the New Moon.

✴ What This Lunation Means for You

Find your Rising sign in this list to discover which House the Moon is in for you (see page 16 for a quick guide): Aries – 7th House; Taurus – 6th House; Gemini – 5th House; Cancer – 4th House; Leo – 3rd House; Virgo – 2nd House; Libra – 1st House; Scorpio – 12th House; Sagittarius – 11th House; Capricorn – 10th House; Aquarius – 9th House; Pisces – 8th House.

✴ The Path to Love

Do you want to attract more love into your life? Try this magical method recommended to me by white witch Francesca De Grandis for my book *Cosmic Love*.

Take six red roses, or six stems of your favourite flower. Walk a couple of streets away from your house and drop one rose. Drop four more on your way back home, then drop the sixth at your door. While you do this, chant out loud or silently: 'This is a path of love. My true love will find me.' You've now given your true love a path by which to find you!

New Moon Wishes and Intentions

What are you manifesting this New Moon? Before you make your list of dreams and desires, visit moonmessages.com/ diarymeditations and listen to the Moon meditation for this month. This will enable you to think from the heart – the best place to be. Then go through your list and 'feel' each wish as real, or feel the feeling of it being fulfilled.

_____

_____

_____

_____

_____

_____

_____

_____

_____

_____

_____

✳ Questions to Ask at This New Moon

Do I believe that I'm worthy of love? If you struggle to answer 'yes' to this question, write 'I am worthy of love' in the space below and repeat the words to yourself every day.

_____

_____

_____

_____

In which areas of my life am I giving as much as I'm taking?

_____

_____

_____

_____

Where in my life am I concerned with what really matters as much as I am with superficial matters?

_____

_____

_____

_____

OCTOBER WEEK 42

12 MONDAY

13 TUESDAY

14 WEDNESDAY

Mercury goes retrograde (until 3 November).

15 THURSDAY

 ♎

Super New Moon
London   20:31
Los Angeles   12:31
New York   15:31

FRIDAY 16

● ♎ ♏

Super New Moon
Sydney   06:31

SATURDAY 17

● ♏

SUNDAY 18

THIS WEEK

Mercury goes retrograde in Scorpio on Wednesday, so be
sure to back up your computer files beforehand.

OCTOBER WEEK 43

. . . .

19 MONDAY

. . . .

20 TUESDAY

. . . .

21 WEDNESDAY

. . . .

22 THURSDAY

. . . .

 Friday 23

What are you grateful for right now?

 Saturday 24

Sunday 25

This Week

This week is good for love and money matters,
thanks to some harmonious Venus links as
we move through the waxing cycle.

November

We're hurtling towards the end of the year and big things are happening this month. Mars retrograde ends, so it should be easier to move forward again. In addition comes another of the Jupiter–Pluto conjunctions that have characterized 2020. Pluto is all about detoxing, so tap into the energy by decluttering your house, your life, your diet, your Facebook friends list and so on.

Energies will build through the month as we approach the next eclipse season. Remember to live consciously – it's

Full Moon in Taurus		
London	31 October	14:49
1 November	1 November	01:49
Los Angeles	31 October	07:49
New York	31 October	10:49
Super New Moon in Scorpio		
London	15 November	05:07
Sydney	15 November	16:07
Los Angeles	14 November	21:07
New York	15 November	00:07

so important, especially at times like this! A pre-end-of-year clear-out could work wonders for your 2021. As usual, the beginning of the month is the time to practise gratitude and decide on your biggest aim for the coming weeks.

M	T	W	T	F	S	S
					31 ◯	1
2	3	4	5	6	7	8 ◑
9	10	11	12	13	14	15 ⬤
16	17	18	19	20	21	22 ◑
23	24	25	26	27	28	29
30 ◯						

~ Things to do this month ~

1. Declutter. Detox. Give it up!
2. Resolve an upset or struggle with a win–win outcome.
3. Forgive someone and move on without looking back.

Full Moon in Taurus

It's a Blue Moon, a Full Moon and a Micromoon, too!

London	31 October	14:49
Sydney	1 November	01:49
Los Angeles	31 October	07:49
New York	31 October	10:49

This Full Moon promises to be a super-exciting time – in fact, some people might be finding it rather too thrilling and changeable. It takes place pretty much on Uranus, the electrical planet of awakenings and turnarounds, so the stage is set for some high vibrations. It's also a Blue Moon, or the second Full Moon in a calendar month

The next Full Moon, on 30 November, is an eclipse, but I think it's fair to say that the intensity of the eclipse season starts to pick up here. What in your life do you want to evolve from? What have you outgrown? Where in your life do you need to be liberated? These are the areas in which you can expect to be 'vibrating' at a higher rate this week.

The one mitigating factor is that this is a Micromoon, meaning that the Full Moon coincides with apogee, i.e. when the Moon is the furthest She gets from Earth during

Her orbit (so the opposite of a Supermoon). Micromoons and Supermoons are more astronomical than astrological events; however, it could be argued that the Moon being at apogee somehow turns down the volume. Let's wait and see this week!

✳ What This Lunation Means for You

Find your Rising sign in this list to discover which House the Moon is in for you (see page 16 for a quick guide): Aries – 2nd House; Taurus – 1st House; Gemini – 12th House; Cancer – 11th House; Leo – 10th House; Virgo – 9th House; Libra – 8th House; Scorpio – 7th House; Sagittarius – 6th House; Capricorn – 5th House; Aquarius – 4th House; Pisces – 3rd House.

✳ The Truth Is...

This is a great time for an exercise that comes from the cognitive behavioural school of thought: The Full Moon + Uranus = the chance to wake up! So, how about using the Full Moon as a way to wake up from some of your fears? Fill out the blanks below:

What I fear is _____

The truth is _____

What I fear is _____

The truth is _____

What I fear is _____

The truth is _____

Full Moon Forgiveness List

Full Moon is an important time for forgiveness, to practise gratitude and to release negativity. What do you need to let go of this month? Who do you need to forgive? What or whom do you need to practise gratitude for?

Visit moonmessages.com/diarymeditations to listen to the Moon meditation for this month, ideally before you make your list below. This will enable you to write from the heart.

_____

_____

_____

_____

_____

_____

_____

_____

_____

_____

ᛧ Questions to Ask at This Full Moon

Do my finances need radical change, and if so, what am I going to do about it?

_____

_____

_____

_____

Do I need to stop being clingy or jealous? With/of whom?

_____

_____

_____

_____

Have I been lazy or overly self-indulgent this month? Make a list of any times this has occurred.

_____

_____

_____

_____

OCTOBER WEEK 44

....

26 MONDAY   ♓︎○

....

27 TUESDAY   ♓︎○

....

28 WEDNESDAY   ♓︎♈︎○

....

29 THURSDAY   ♈︎○

....

○♈︎♉︎   FRIDAY 30

○♉︎   SATURDAY 31

Full Moon
London   14:49
Los Angeles   07:49
New York   10:49

Festivals of Samhain (UK/USA) and Beltane (Aus)

○♉︎   SUNDAY 1

Full Moon
Sydney   01:49

THIS WEEK

*Samhain, which celebrates the end of the harvest season
and the beginning of winter, is marked in the northern
hemisphere, while Beltane, marking the peak of spring and
the beginning of summer, is celebrated Down Under.*

NOVEMBER WEEK 45

2 MONDAY ♉♊○

3 TUESDAY ♊○

Mercury retrograde ends.

4 WEDNESDAY ♊♋○

5 THURSDAY ♋○

 FRIDAY 6

SATURDAY 7

SUNDAY 8

What are you grateful for right now?

THIS WEEK

*The last Mercury retrograde cycle of the year ends on
Tuesday. If you're been waiting to book a holiday, or buy
a new phone or car, wait until the end of the week.*

Super New Moon in Scorpio

Get clear on what you want and then go for it!

London	15 November	05:07
Sydney	15 November	16:07
Los Angeles	14 November	21:07
New York	15 November	00:07

Most of the energies this week are friendly and supportive, so this a great time just to go for it. We have the last Jupiter–Pluto connection of the year, so this has the potential to be a big (Jupiter) and transformative (Pluto) week for you. Pluto is the planet that transforms from the inside out – sometimes the effects are more psychological and less tangible, but they can be paradigm-changing all the same.

This week's Super New Moon in Scorpio adds fuel to the fire. Pluto is the modern planet associated with Scorpio (the traditional planet is Mars), and we have the New Moon in Pluto's sign as Pluto (the planet of casting out that which no longer serves you) connects with the planet of luck, Jupiter (which always amplifies matters). If that wasn't enough, Mars, the planet of determination, ends its retrograde cycle.

Every New Moon is about manifesting, but this New Moon is associated with Pluto and Pluto is the magician of the zodiac. So, in the words of Abraham-Hicks: 'Think about what you want, don't think about what you don't want.' Make this your magical mantra this month.

Note that Venus and Pluto clash after the New Moon, so there could be some issues simmering around love, money and/or obsession. Remember to live consciously. The Moon goes Void of Course after the New Moon, so wait at least 11 hours after the New Moon to make your wishes.

⚸ What This Lunation Means for You

Find your Rising sign in this list to discover which House the Moon is in for you (see page 16 for a quick guide): Aries – 8th House; Taurus – 7th House; Gemini – 6th House; Cancer – 5th House; Leo – 4th House; Virgo – 3rd House; Libra – 2nd House; Scorpio – 1st House; Sagittarius – 12th House; Capricorn – 11th House; Aquarius – 10th House; Pisces – 9th House.

⚸ Welcome Kali

The Hindu Goddess Kali is most often associated with Scorpio and the New Moon, and the corresponding Jupiter–Pluto action make it an amazing time to connect with her.

She's said to be the most misunderstood Goddess, but is actually a part of the Divine Feminine or the Divine Mother. We shouldn't fear her, just because she's powerful! Rather, Kali can give us the energy and courage to face up to and see off our fears. Visit moonmessages.com/kali2020 to listen to the free Kali meditation I've recorded for you.

New Moon Wishes and Intentions

What are you manifesting this New Moon? Before you make your list of dreams and desires, visit moonmessages.com/diarymeditations and listen to the Moon meditation for this month. This will enable you to think from the heart – the best place to be. Then go through your list and 'feel' each wish as real, or feel the feeling of it being fulfilled.

_____

_____

_____

_____

_____

_____

_____

_____

_____

_____

_____

✳ Questions to Ask at This New Moon

Do I need to reconnect with my sexuality, and if so, how am I going to do that?

_____

_____

_____

_____

Do I love myself, including my shadow side? Honour any parts you don't love.

_____

_____

_____

_____

Do I need to release any toxic emotions? What are they?

_____

_____

_____

_____

NOVEMBER WEEK 46

9 MONDAY

10 TUESDAY

11 WEDNESDAY

12 THURSDAY

 FRIDAY 13

 SATURDAY 14

Super New Moon
Los Angeles   21:07

Mars retrograde ends.

 SUNDAY 15

Super New Moon
London   05:07
Sydney   16:07
New York   00:07

THIS WEEK

The Scorpio New Moon is the ideal time to ditch a grudge.
Remember that the Moon goes Void of Course after the New
Moon, so wait until Sunday evening to make your wishes.

NOVEMBER WEEK 47

....

16 MONDAY

....

17 TUESDAY

....

18 WEDNESDAY

....

19 THURSDAY

....

 FRIDAY 20

 SATURDAY 21

SUNDAY 22

What are you grateful for right now?

THIS WEEK

Venus, the planet of love, clashes with Pluto this week, so don't be surprised if you feel a bit unloved or unloving – hopefully it will only be a fleeting feeling!

NOVEMBER WEEK 48

23 MONDAY

24 TUESDAY

25 WEDNESDAY

26 THURSDAY

○♍︎♉   FRIDAY **27**

○♉   SATURDAY **28**

○♉♊   SUNDAY **29**

THIS WEEK

If you want to make a major change connected to love
or money, this is the week to manifest it. Remember to
'feel' the feeling of the wish already fulfilled.

December

We're in another eclipse season, which began with the Full Moon eclipse on 30 November. Now is a great time to detox and let go, and the super-powerful New Moon eclipse on 14 December is a good time to start thinking about your intentions for 2021. Just as you might plan your week on a Sunday night, now is the time to plan for the coming year. For best results, do this on the night of the New Moon.

This month also sees Jupiter move into Aquarius and a Jupiter–Saturn alignment, so the year should end on a

Full Moon eclipse in Gemini		
London	30 November	09:29
Sydney	30 November	20:29
Los Angeles	30 November	01:29
New York	30 November	04:29
New Moon eclipse in Sagittarius		
London	14 December	16:16
Sydney	15 December	03:16
Los Angeles	14 December	08:16
New York	14 December	11:16

steady, happy, 'lessons learned' note. During the first week of the month, remember to think about what you're grateful for in your life and decide on the most important thing you want to achieve in the weeks ahead.

M	T	W	T	F	S	S
30 ○	1	2	3	4	5	6
7	8 ◑	9	10	11	12	13
14 ●	15	16	17	18	19	20
21 ◐	22	23	24	25	26	27
28	29	30 ○	31			

∼ Things to do this month ∼

1. Think about the lessons 2020 taught you.
2. Make a list of everything you've been grateful for in 2020.
3. Make a to-do list for your personal and professional life in 2021.

Full Moon Eclipse in Gemini

Clear your head and think positive thoughts.

London	30 November	09:29
Sydney	30 November	20:29
Los Angeles	30 November	01:29
New York	30 November	04:29

This looks like a potentially amazing week: we enter the last eclipse season of the year and just afterwards comes a link between Saturn and Mercury, the planet that rules Gemini.

Gemini is the changeable sign with a feeling of being all over the place at times. On the one hand it feels like a lot might be said this week, and in fact there's a danger of saying too much. However, once you've expressed yourself (with integrity, of course) what follows should be positive. It's also a very good week for signing a contract or making a deal.

The Full Moon eclipse in Gemini is also an amazing time to clear your head, so think positively and let go of any arguments. This isn't to say that you shouldn't ever think negatively. We all need to process our thoughts and feelings, and the Full Moon is the best time to do that. Gemini is all about thoughts, and thoughts and feelings are usually intertwined. However, once you've worked through them, let them go. You can repeat 'The Truth Is...' exercise from last month's New Moon in Taurus (see page 213) to replace any fear with a fact. Some things are worth letting go. Contemplate that idea this week.

This lunar eclipse is in a mutable sign (along with Virgo, Sagittarius and Pisces, the mutable signs are known for assisting us through times of transition). That makes this an especially good time to think about what you're holding on to and why, and whether it's necessary.

⚹ What This Lunation Means for You

Find your Rising sign in this list to discover which House the Moon is in for you (see page 16 for a quick guide): Aries – 3rd House; Taurus – 2nd House; Gemini – 1st House; Cancer – 12th House; Leo – 11th House; Virgo – 10th House; Libra – 9th House; Scorpio – 8th House; Sagittarius – 7th House; Capricorn – 6th House; Aquarius – 5th House; Pisces – 4th House.

⚹ Just say 'Auuummm'

One of the best ways to work with the energies this week is to meditate, so if you haven't been keeping up your practice, now is the time to get back into it. Just sit quietly and chant 'Auuummm...', the phonetic spelling of 'Om', a yogic chant that represents the sound of the Universe. Alternatively, YouTube has a number of guided meditations that you can listen to, including a selection from Deepak Chopra.

Full Moon Forgiveness List

Full Moon is an important time for forgiveness, to practise gratitude and to release negativity. What do you need to let go of this month? Who do you need to forgive? What or whom do you need to practise gratitude for?

Visit moonmessages.com/diarymeditations to listen to the Moon meditation for this month, ideally before you make your list below. This will enable you to write from the heart.

_____

_____

_____

_____

_____

_____

_____

_____

_____

✳ Questions to Ask at This Full Moon

Have I been superficial and glossing over other people's feelings? List any occasions when this has been the case.

_____

_____

_____

_____

What more could I read, listen to or watch to expand my mind?

_____

_____

_____

_____

Have I been feeling restless, and if so, what do I need to address?

_____

_____

_____

_____

....

30 MONDAY

Full Moon eclipse

London	09:29
Sydney	20:29
Los Angeles	01:29
New York	04:29

....

1 TUESDAY

....

2 WEDNESDAY

....

3 THURSDAY

....

◐ ♋ ♌   FRIDAY 4

◐ ♌   SATURDAY 5

◐ ♌ ♍   SUNDAY 6

THIS WEEK

We move from the Full Moon eclipse straight into the Waning Cycle so b-r-e-a-t-h-e out! Schedule in some downtime this week if you can; otherwise make time next week.

December Week 50

7 Monday

8 Tuesday

What are you grateful for right now?

9 Wednesday

10 Thursday

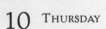

 FRIDAY 11

 SATURDAY 12

 SUNDAY 13

THIS WEEK

We're now in the third and final eclipse season of the year so make sure you work it! Hint: start to decide what you want for 2021.

New Moon Eclipse in Sagittarius

It's the penultimate lunation of 2020.

London	14 December	16:16
Sydney	15 December	03:16
Los Angeles	14 December	08:16
New York	14 December	11:16

So much is happening this week! We have a New Moon, an eclipse, Saturn moving from Capricorn into Aquarius, Jupiter moving into Aquarius and a rare (once every 12 years) Jupiter–Saturn conjunction.

When energies stack up this way, all we can do is be aware and live consciously. The New Moon eclipse makes this a super-powerful week, so be sure to invest some real energy into your New Moon wishes and intentions. However, the Moon goes Void of Course after the New Moon, so wait at least 12 hours to make your wish list.

With two outer planets, Jupiter and Saturn, changing signs, it's a turnaround week for everyone, no matter their Star sign or Rising sign, so stay awake!

If you like to work with the archangels, this is the time to tune in to Archangel Raguel, who is associated with the sign of Sagittarius. Raguel is known for bringing harmony and balance, so call on him if you're having trouble seeing the funny side of a situation, if you'd like to take your life in a more adventurous direction or you need help to resolve a relationship conflict.

✳ What This Lunation Means for You

Find your Rising sign in this list to discover which House the Moon is in for you (see page 16 for a quick guide): Aries – 9th House; Taurus – 8th House; Gemini – 7th House; Cancer – 6th House; Leo – 5th House; Virgo – 4th House; Libra – 3rd House; Scorpio – 2nd House; Sagittarius – 1st House; Capricorn – 12th House; Aquarius – 11th House; Pisces – 10th House.

✳ You Were Born Magical

As the year comes to an end, I'd like to remind you that you are magical. When you look back through this diary, can you see where your dreams have come true? Can you see how you've managed to consciously create your life?

The fact is that where we put our intention, energy flows and magic happens. Where your wishes didn't manifest, think about whether or not you really believed in your ability to make your dream come true. Were you too impatient or too desperate, or did you focus on what you didn't want instead of 'feeling' the feeling of the wish fulfilled? Just remember that everything appears at the perfect time, stunningly aligned with your soul's needs.

New Moon Wishes and Intentions

What are you manifesting this New Moon? Before you make your list of dreams and desires, visit moonmessages.com/ diarymeditations and listen to the Moon meditation for this month. This will enable you to think from the heart – the best place to be. Then go through your list and 'feel' each wish as real, or feel the feeling of it being fulfilled.

_____

_____

_____

_____

_____

_____

_____

_____

_____

_____

_____

_____

⽊ Questions to Ask at This New Moon

This year, have I lived life as the adventure it is? If not, how can I be more adventurous next year?

_____

_____

_____

_____

What are my travel plans for the year ahead? Write a wish list.

_____

_____

_____

_____

Could further study improve my personal or professional life? If so, what and how?

_____

_____

_____

_____

DECEMBER WEEK 51

....

14 MONDAY

New Moon eclipse
London   16:16
Los Angeles   08:16
New York   11:16

♐

....

15 TUESDAY

New Moon eclipse
Sydney   03:16

♐♑

....

16 WEDNESDAY

♑ ◖

....

17 THURSDAY

♑♒

....

 FRIDAY 18

 SATURDAY 19

● ♓ SUNDAY 20

THIS WEEK

*Expect the New Moon eclipse to bring energies
that are a little over the top. Use them or lose
them! It's the last eclipse of the year.*

DECEMBER WEEK 52

....

21 MONDAY

Winter Solstice/Yule (UK/USA); Summer Solstice/Litha (Aus)
....

22 TUESDAY

....

23 WEDNESDAY

....

24 THURSDAY

○♉   FRIDAY 25

○♉♊   SATURDAY 26

○♊   SUNDAY 27

THIS WEEK

It's the Winter Solstice, or midwinter, in the northern hemisphere, while Down Under celebrates the Summer Solstice, the day with the longest period of light.

Full Moon in Cancer

Practise gratitude for all that has been good in 2020.

London	30 December	03:28
Sydney	30 December	14:28
Los Angeles	29 December	19:28
New York	29 December	22:28

So here we are at the end of the year, with a Full Moon to send us into 2021. How was 2020 for you? Do you love your life a little more now than you did at the beginning of the year? If so, mission accomplished! And if not, then there is always 2021 to get in tune with the Moon. Remember that the Earth is a school of manifestation, and we're here to learn how to consciously create our lives by getting clear on what we want and releasing self-doubt.

If life feels confusing just now, blame Venus and Neptune; these two planets are clashing this week, so there's the potential for a lot of confusion around love and abundance. If you're unsure about the best way forward when it comes to love or money, ask Archangel Gabriel for guidance.

The good news is that, wherever you live, what was so perplexing at the start of the week is likely to be more comprehensible by 1 January. The New Year begins with the Moon in Leo, so show 2021 what you've got!

Before the week is out, use the power of the Full Moon to release anything from 2020 you want to leave behind, and then go into a frenzy of gratitude for all that's good in your life! Gratitude will raise your vibration and that, after all, is the aim of the game!

⚷ What This Lunation Means for You

Find your Rising sign in this list to discover which House the Moon is in for you (see page 16 for a quick guide): Aries – 4th House; Taurus – 3rd House; Gemini – 2nd House; Cancer – 1st House; Leo – 12th House; Virgo – 11th House; Libra – 10th House; Scorpio – 9th House; Sagittarius – 8th House; Capricorn – 7th House; Aquarius – 6th House; Pisces – 5th House.

⚷ Thank You, Universe, Thank You

Sit quietly with your phone turned off at a time when you won't be disturbed, and just breathe. When you're feeling grounded, bring to mind someone or something you're truly grateful for. Hold their image in your mind while you continue breathing deeply and say, 'Thank you, Universe, thank you'. Repeat this process for the three people or things you're most grateful for in your life.

You were born magical, but you need to release your magic by practising gratitude for all that you have. Remember to do this at least as often as you think about what you want to create for yourself, on the night of every Full Moon and New Year's Eve. It can really work wonders!

Full Moon Forgiveness List

Full Moon is an important time for forgiveness, to practise gratitude and to release negativity. What do you need to let go of this month? Who do you need to forgive? What or whom do you need to practise gratitude for?

Visit moonmessages.com/diarymeditations to listen to the Moon meditation for this month, ideally before you make your list below. This will enable you to write from the heart.

_____

_____

_____

_____

_____

_____

_____

_____

_____

_____

⚵ Questions to Ask at This Full Moon

What do I need to release from my life – from 2020 or any time at all?

_____

_____

_____

_____

Is there anyone in my family I need to make peace with?

_____

_____

_____

_____

What are my top three aims for 2021?

_____

_____

_____

_____

DECEMBER 2020 WEEK 1

. . . .

28 MONDAY

♊︎ ○

. . . .

29 TUESDAY

Full Moon
Los Angeles   19:28
New York   22:28

. . . .

30 WEDNESDAY

♋︎ ○

Full Moon
London   03:28
Sydney   14:28

. . . .

31 THURSDAY

. . . .

◐ ♌   FRIDAY 1

◐ ♌   SATURDAY 2

◐ ♌ ♍   SUNDAY 3

THIS WEEK

The year ahead looks set to bring much change and a few unexpected curveballs. Continue to set your intentions at New Moon, and release and practise gratitude at Full Moon, and you'll sail through it with ease and grace!

JANUARY

M	T	W	T	F	S	S
				1	2	3
4	5	6	7	8	9	10
11	12	13	14	15	16	17
18	19	20	21	22	23	24
25	26	27	28	29	30	31

FEBRUARY

M	T	W	T	F	S	S
1	2	3	4	5	6	7
8	9	10	11	12	13	14
15	16	17	18	19	20	21
22	23	24	25	26	27	28

MARCH

M	T	W	T	F	S	S
1	2	3	4	5	6	7
8	9	10	11	12	13	14
15	16	17	18	19	20	21
22	23	24	25	26	27	28
29	30	31				

APRIL

M	T	W	T	F	S	S
			1	2	3	4
5	6	7	8	9	10	11
12	13	14	15	16	17	18
19	20	21	22	23	24	25
26	27	28	29	30		

MAY

M	T	W	T	F	S	S
					1	2
3	4	5	6	7	8	9
10	11	12	13	14	15	16
17	18	19	20	21	22	23
24	25	26	27	28	29	30
31						

JUNE

M	T	W	T	F	S	S
	1	2	3	4	5	6
7	8	9	10	11	12	13
14	15	16	17	18	19	20
21	22	23	24	25	26	27
28	29	30				

JULY

M	T	W	T	F	S	S
		1	2	3	4	
5	6	7	8	9	10	11
12	13	14	15	16	17	18
19	20	21	22	23	24	25
26	27	28	29	30	31	

AUGUST

M	T	W	T	F	S	S
						1
2	3	4	5	6	7	8
9	10	11	12	13	14	15
16	17	18	19	20	21	22
23	24	25	26	27	28	29
30	31					

SEPTEMBER

M	T	W	T	F	S	S
		1	2	3	4	5
6	7	8	9	10	11	12
13	14	15	16	17	18	19
20	21	22	23	24	25	26
27	28	29	30			

OCTOBER

M	T	W	T	F	S	S
				1	2	3
4	5	6	7	8	9	10
11	12	13	14	15	16	17
18	19	20	21	22	23	24
25	26	27	28	29	30	31

NOVEMBER

M	T	W	T	F	S	S
1	2	3	4	5	6	7
8	9	10	11	12	13	14
15	16	17	18	19	20	21
22	23	24	25	26	27	28
29	30					

DECEMBER

M	T	W	T	F	S	S
		1	2	3	4	5
6	7	8	9	10	11	12
13	14	15	16	17	18	19
20	21	22	23	24	25	26
27	28	29	30	31		

Notes

Notes

ABOUT THE AUTHOR

George Petting

Yasmin Boland began her career as a freelance journalist with a passion for writing and astrology. Owing to various cosmic turns of events, these passions turned into her profession and she's now one of the most widely read astrology writers on the planet, with columns published all over the world.

Yasmin loves all astrology but has a special interest in the Moon, specifically in New and Full Moons. At her website moonology.com you can read her Daily Moon Message, plus her weekly, monthly and annual horoscopes; she also has a flourishing Facebook community. Yasmin's books include *Moonology*, *Astrology Made Easy* and *The Mercury Retrograde Book*. She was born in Germany, grew up in Tasmania and so far has lived in Australia, France and England.

 f yasminbolandsmoonology

𝕏 @yasminboland

◉ @planetyasminboland

www.yasminboland.com
www.moonology.com